THE GREEN LADDER

THE GREEN LADDER

PARADIGM SHIFTS

TOWARD A KINGDOM LIFESTYLE

BY STEVE SHAW

DEDICATION

It is my highest honor to dedicate this book to the Vineyard Christian Fellowship of Grants Pass, Oregon, where I have pastored for the last thirty-four years. Your love for the King, your passion for His presence, and your willingness to take risks and follow the King wherever He would lead us is what made this book possible. Through you I've come to understand what the apostle Paul meant when he told the Philippian church you are my joy and my crown. God's love shining through each of you has given me the opportunity to pastor a church I never dreamed could exist this side of Heaven. Thanks for your trust and support. I love you all so much.

ACKNOWLEDGEMENTS

To my wife Midge—I couldn't have asked for a greater or more supportive wife. Thanks for going after every misused comma and semicolon in the book.

Gaylord Enns—thank you for not only encouraging me in this project, but for also coaching me along the way. You've influenced my life more than you'll ever know.

Doug Perkins and Doug Thomas—you two have been instrumental in fashioning my life and the Vineyard Christian Fellowship where we co-labor. The unique blending of our gifts has been a launching pad to equip the saints and release them into their destinies. I will always treasure your counsel, support, faithfulness, and dedication to me and to the vision the Lord has placed before us.

Christina Files—thanks for believing in me and seeing the potential of *The Green Ladder*. Your command of language, your knowledge of Scripture, and your sensitivity to future readers have worked together with your incredible editing skills to take this book to another level. It's been a real joy and pleasure working with you.

Evelyn Sawtelle and the army of intercessors—your unceasing

prayers have carried me along from beginning to end. The vision has stayed clear, the revelations have remained fresh, and the strength I've needed has been supplied. Your labor in the Heavens has given birth to this amazing project in the earth. Thanks!

ENDORSEMENTS

The Green Ladder provides a fresh look into how the body of Christ can begin to walk in their God-given identity. When we learn to embrace all that Jesus provided for us, we learn to co-labor with God. Cultivating this Kingdom mindset helps to bring an ease and grace as we step into a Kingdom lifestyle that changes the world around us.

Bill Johnson
Senior Pastor
Bethel Church, Redding, California
Author *When Heaven Invades Earth* and
Face to Face With God

In this hour the Spirit of God is beckoning an entire generation to embrace a Kingdomgospel and a supernatural King. In his book, *The Green Ladder*, Steve Shaw describes three major paradigm shifts that are necessary prerequisites for the body of Christ to reach a place of maturity. If you're tired of fake fruit and want a taste of a Christianity that's real, this book is for you!

Jeff Jansen
Founder of Global Fire Ministries International &
Global Fire Church & World Miracle Center
Nashville, Tennessee
Author *Glory Rising*
www.globalfireministries.com

The Green Ladder may sound like an unpublished writing from Dr. Seuss, but is in fact packed with vital information concerning the Kingdom of God. For too long those who have failed to manifest any evidence of the King's presence, power, or purity have held the term "kingdom" hostage. Steve Shaw puts the trumpet to his mouth and sounds the alarm, calling the Church to rise to her calling and destiny. While many in these days look for the coming of the Lord, few seem to be concerned with hastening His coming. *"This gospel of the Kingdom shall be preached...then shall the end come"* (Matthew 24:14 KJV). I don't suggest you read this book because you will be held accountable on that great day. Instead, read it, absorb it, pray it, and practice it. Together, we can see His Kingdom come.

David Ravenhill
Itinerant Teacher
Author *They Drank from the River and Died in the Wilderness*
Siloam Springs, Arkansas

Steve Shaw is addressing a very crucial subject in this must-read book. This book is a God-given gift to the body of Christ, as there appears to either be a deficit of revelation on this topic, or of writers who are willing to write about it. If your prayer has been, "God, what do you think when you think of me?" then I both challenge and encourage you to read with a ready heart—ready for information, impartation, and transformation.

Pastor Jackson Senyonga
President/Founder of Christian Life Ministries USA
Christian Life Church, Uganda, Africa

Relationships define our identities and destinies. The degree of influence and authority we have is based on the levels of relationship we have, first with God and then with one another, because the kingdom of God is built on relationships. Steve Shaw clearly lays out for us the importance of properly realigning ourselves with the presence and intended purposes of God. We often strive for what already belongs to us, thus trying to take by force what has been given by inheritance from our heavenly Father. Steve understands the importance that our destinations (destinies) are in the Father's presence where our identities have been secured. I find this book a refreshing encouragement and challenge to contend for authenticity and genuineness in our Christian walk. Steve, in a provoking, yet pastoral and honest nudge, has directed the reader to a fresh revelation of personal and corporate possibilities when we co-labor with God.

Doug Stringer
Founder/President
Somebody Cares America Int'l.
Turning Point Ministries International

Steve writes not from his head, though he is very intelligent, but from the heart of his experience in leading a group of Jesus followers into being the church that Jesus promised we could all be. The local church Steve has pastored for 34 years is living proof that what he says in his book works. We have ministered in hundreds of churches all over the world, and we can honestly say Steve's is one of the minority we went into for the first time and found a majority of the people there actually living out the three paradigm shifts he so accurately describes. We believe the whole church, every believer, is mandated by God to be naturally supernatural, destroying the works of the devil and advancing the kingdom of God. And we believe *The Green Ladder* will give leaders what they need to move their people into that reality. We highly recommend this book for everyone who is hungering to see the "more" of Christianity they find in the Bible.

Bill and Carol Dew
Dewnamis Ministries, Inc.
www.dewnamis.com

My heart resonated deeply with the message in *The Green Ladder*. The topics that Steve discusses are so much a part of my life message that I feel like we have been on a similar journey. I have fed myself from his material. He is a talented writer, and his book will generate an encouraging, spirited conversation that will sharpen the body of Christ. Every believer desperately needs to hear this message.

Larry Lane
Director of Kingdom Catalyst
Neighborhood Church, Chico, California
kingdomc.org

You are a child of God. That means that to do anything below what you were created to do will bore you. Your supernatural origin and the legacy of triumph that makes up the Christian faith demands that you do something great with your life.

—Mario Murillo, *Critical Mass*

CONTENTS

Step Three: Co-Laboring With God

FOREWORD

I have had the privilege of knowing Steve Shaw and his wife, Midge, for over forty years. They were part of the hippie movement of the 70s, but on the day I met them, they had experienced that amazing spiritual rebirth that Jesus described to Nicodemus—*"I tell you the truth, no one can see the kingdom of God unless he is born again."*

I've watched them mature into very effective and fruitful leaders—now seasoned through decades of productive pastoral and missionary ministry. The truths Steve Shaw shares in *The Green Ladder* have been proven and can be seen in the congregation they serve. It bubbles with life—a place of restoration and healing for so many.

But why a "ladder?" Ladders are ancient and wonderful inventions. They enable us to access something that would otherwise be out of our reach. That is the Green Ladder! The insights contained in this book are kingdom truths, not far from us, yet above us in the heavenly realm in which Jesus reigns. This ladder will be a tool that helps you bring that heavenly treasure into your life and the life of your congregation.

Read it and be changed!

Gaylord Enns
Author of *Love Revolution:*
Rediscovering the Lost Command of Jesus

INTRODUCTION

"Insanity: doing the same thing over and over again but expecting different results."—
Albert Einstein

As a pastor I've not only known about this quote; I've actually lived it out—again, and again, and again. I have even attempted to prove it wrong, believing that if I just tried a little harder, I would get different results. Yet in the end I was always proven wrong and was left feeling completely frustrated. I have learned, however, that frustration is one of God's best tools.

In your hands is the fruit of my labor—*The Green Ladder: Paradigm Shifts for a Kingdom Lifestyle.* The content for it comes out of my own life and the church where I have had the privilege of pastoring for 34 years. Many of those years were years of insanity and frustration where I had to painfully discover for myself that *"unless the Lord builds the house, its builders labor in vain"* (Psalm 127:1 NIV).

The Green Ladder is a book about transition and change. It's about unlearning, relearning, and looking at the Scriptures through a different lens. It's a book about paradigm shifts—shifts that do far more than simply tweak our current ways of thinking. These shifts actually alter our perspective, worldview, and destinies. They are the kind of shifts that bring about renewed minds and transformations in individuals, churches, cities, and nations.

As my leadership team and I led our congregation into a season of prayer, the Lord prophetically gave us a promise that we would become a spiritual icebreaker. An icebreaker is a ship that slowly plows through ice-covered waters making it possible for other ships to follow. The prophetic word didn't excite me too much at first, because it sounded like a lot of hard, slow work. I finally resolved that if that was the destiny the Lord had for our fellowship, then so be it. It was a dirty job, but somebody had to do it, and we finally said yes.

Though I had no idea how long it would take to break through the religious ice when we began, we just kept at it—year after year after year after year. Every now and then, we would see small breakthroughs that encouraged us onward, but for the most part it was a long process of ramming into the ice again and again until it cracked open a little more and we moved on ahead.

It probably took us seven or eight years to finally break through the ice and come into the open waters of the Spirit. This book is the story of how the Lord prepared, equipped, and enabled us to enter into our destiny of breaking through the frozen waters. Once through, I felt the Lord impress upon me that other churches would be able to get through the icy waters in a much shorter time because of what we had done. I actually feel in my spirit that other fellowships can come through this opened channel in a period of two years or less.

Shortly before I started writing, the Lord gave us another promise for our fellowship. He told us He was going to transform us from an icebreaker ship to a tugboat. A tugboat *is a boat used to maneuver, primarily by towing or pushing, other vessels in harbors, over the open sea or through rivers and canals.*[1] The unique thing about tugboats is that they don't take control of another vessel. They just assist them so they can get out of the harbor, through the channels and storms, and can arrive at their given destinations. I pray that this book acts like a tugboat for you and pulls you into a deeper revelation of God's plan for your life.

My hope is that you enjoy *The Green Ladder* as much as I have enjoyed this process of transformation. Embracing the paradigm shifts this book presents has proven to be fruitful, powerful, and full of glory.

THE GREEN LADDER

CHAPTER 1

I WANT YOU TO WRITE A BOOK

It all started back in 2007 when I awoke at 3:00 o'clock one morning. I'll never know why the Lord likes to talk to me at this time. I've come to tell myself that this is the time He visits His favorites. What I heard that morning wasn't the usual concern that He wanted me to pray about or the revelatory thoughts He often gave me for our fellowship. This word totally shook me out of my sleepy state. The casual and friendly tone of His voice bothered me in light of what He said. It was as if He was simply asking me to *pass the salt*. But what I heard that morning was no "pass the salt." That I can do. No. The words I heard were, *"I want you to write a book."* *"What? Write a book?"* I said to myself.

I couldn't get over the tone of His voice lingering in the air. I wondered if God just sat on a bench one day with Noah and told him, *"I want you to build an ark."* I know it's not really clear in the Bible, but I kind of imagine the manifest presence of God bursting in on Noah followed by a few *fear nots* and then the Lord's best Darth Vader voice booming, **"NOAH, BUILD ME AN ARK!!!"**

I know what you're thinking. This is no ark. This is a simple book. Yeah, but to me, this book might as well be an ark. Sure, I've read hundreds of books, and they're great things. But how could I write one? My writing skills included such great feats as emails, birthday cards, sermon notes, and the famous one-page Christmas letter. I didn't know anything about writing and my wife, an English professor at a local college, has told me I don't even speak English. I speak American! Wait a minute. That's it! He came to the right bed but woke up the wrong person. My wife's supposed to write a book, not me.

"I want you to write a book." It was like He replayed the tape, and I heard it all over again. In my heart I felt He was neither asking me a question nor giving me a booming command. It was simply my Father and my friend speaking to me with the confidence that He had in me. He actually believed in me and that what He had worked within my spirit for many years could now be brought forth and given to others. For a brief moment, I rested in His loving presence feeling humbled, honored, and terrified as I whispered to myself, *"I'm going to write a book."*

Whoa! Note the last sentence said "a brief moment." That moment was quickly up, and I came back down. *"Write a book! Write a book about what?"* I mumbled into the darkness.

His voice came again. Though it wasn't the familiar language of the Bible, in my spirit I knew and understood exactly what He meant. *"Write a book about the three major paradigm shifts I've brought you and your fellowship through."* As soon as those words were spoken, there seemed to be an immediate download into my spirit. In a moment of time, I saw all the changes the Lord had been slowly working in my life since my conversion in 1970 and in the life of the church I have pastored for 33 years. He prompted me to write about three transformational paradigm shifts that I had experienced.

1. Shifting from the *gospel of salvation* to the *gospel of the kingdom*.

2. Shifting from a *sinner/shame-based identity* to a *saint/righteousness-based identity*.

3. Shifting from an *extreme view of God's sovereignty* to *co-laboring with a sovereign God*.

So What's a Paradigm Shift?

A paradigm is simply a pattern or model of thought. We all have hundreds of paradigms we live with everyday that govern our lives, and we give very little thought to them. Most of us weren't taught these paradigms as much as we caught them within the culture we were raised. Paradigms are the glasses we wear, the lenses we see through that shape our worldview. To each of us, our paradigms are very predictable and very right. The problem with having paradigms, though, is that they are usually very hard to change. We often say we're "open-minded," but in practice we're usually not.

Changing our paradigm is called a shift—a paradigm shift. These shifts are essential as we develop as Christians and recover from the paradigms given to us by the world and religious systems. Unfortunately, many of us brought our old, worldly paradigms into

> *We are transformed into His image when we allow our minds to be renewed.*

our Christianity. We have unconsciously thwarted the incredible plan the Lord has for our lives. Without the proper paradigm shifts, we try and create God in our image instead of being created in His image. We are transformed into His image when we allow our minds to be renewed. Our minds are renewed as we experience paradigm shifts that cause us to look at things differently. Paul explains it like this:

> Do not conform any longer to the pattern of this world, but be transformed by the renewing of your mind (Romans 12:2 NIV).

> Don't copy the behavior and customs of this world, but let God transform you into a new person by changing the way you think (Romans 12:2 NLT).

A perfect, historical example of a paradigm shift is when people stopped thinking that the world was flat or bowl shaped to understanding that it is round. People that had a flat-world lens saw the earth (and themselves) as the center of the universe with the sun, moon, and stars moving around them. Explorers were often ruled by fear rather than adventure because they thought it possible to sail off the edge of the earth.

In the beginning of round-world thinking, people began to see the sun as the center of the universe with the earth and everything else rotating around it. This paradigm shift opened the way for many great adventurers and explorers to pursue the unknown without fearing that they might sail over the edge. (For those of you who are already drawing parallels to spirituality, it's interesting to note that some of the greatest resisters of the round-world persuasion were the religious leaders of the day.)

In Acts 10, we find Peter having an incredible paradigm shift that challenged and changed two thousand years of religious customs and traditions in a single afternoon. In this passage we find Peter up on a roof praying and falling into a trance. He then saw a sheet drop from heaven with all kinds of unclean animals on it, and God tells him to kill and eat them. Peter, probably hoping to impress the Lord, responds from his rule-based traditions and states that he's never eaten anything unclean in his life. The Lord then tells him to call nothing unclean that He has cleaned. After this scene plays out before Peter three times, the shift takes place, and Peter metaphorically walks through this newly opened door to minister the gospel to the Gentile nations.

In 1998, there was a great theatrical paradigm shift played out before our eyes in the movie *The Truman Show*. It's a film about a man named Truman Burbank who, unknown to himself, has lived his entire life on an elaborate movie set and is slowly coming to realize there's something more out there that is calling him to break out of his little world. As a young boy, Truman shares with his classmates that he wants to become an explorer one day. His teacher quickly pulls down a map and explains that everything has already been discovered, thus reinforcing Truman's limited view of the world.

Later in the movie, the creator of *The Truman Show* is being interviewed. When asked why Truman hasn't discovered that the world he lives in is not real, the creator responds by saying that we accept the reality of the world we are presented. Because of well-placed props and implanted childhood memories, Truman fears the unknown and remains on the movie set until he's willing to risk it all, face his fears, and allow his paradigm and life to be radically shifted. This movie is such a clear example of how paradigms affect our view of every facet of life.

Spikes and Process

If we could look at a line chart of our life, paradigm shifts would appear like spikes that interrupt our normal, daily rhythm. We move along from day to day at our normal pace and then a *suddenly* happens. A *suddenly* is an instant paradigm shift that changes our perspective and the direction we are headed.

The disciples experienced a *suddenly* on the Day of Pentecost that launched the Church. Saul experienced a *suddenly* on the road to Damascus that transformed a persecutor into a preacher. Philip experienced a

> *A suddenly is an instant paradigm shift that changes our perspective and the direction we are headed in.*
> ～

suddenly when he was translated. It could either be a surprise *suddenly* like Peter's paradigm shift about unclean animals. Or a person could have a *suddenly* after pondering a truth for a long time, like those who suddenly embraced round-world thinking after much contemplation.

In fact, two people could have the same revelation come to them, and it could be a quick *suddenly* to one and a slow *suddenly* to the other. The apostle Paul had a radical encounter one day and immediately believed in the claims of Jesus and His Lordship. C. S. Lewis, on the other hand, considered the claims of Christ and Christianity for a couple of years before the final revelation of the Lordship of Christ came to Him while riding a bus in England. Either way, a spike occurred on the chart of both of their lives and their destinies were forever changed.

But we need more than spikes and paradigm shifts in our lives; we also need process. Process answers the question, *"What do we do with the revelation He's given us?"* John Wimber, founder of the Vineyard movement, coined the simple phrase *"doin' the stuff."* That caused a paradigm shift to occur in my life. Somehow my congregation and I had gotten sidetracked and had slowly become spiritually bushwhacked at our Bible studies.

We were surprised at the revelation we received about how we could live out our faith. We had slowly become *hearers* of the word instead of *doers* of the word. We had convinced ourselves that studying Him was the same as following Him, but that just isn't true. To follow Him takes faith, and faith comes from having a revelation. In the parable of the talents, Jesus doesn't tell the servants, *"Well believed"*; he tells them, *"Well done."*

It may come as a surprise to some, but He's not all that concerned with our doctrines and theologies if they don't lead us to doin' the stuff; and doin' the stuff takes faith, and that's what pleases God (see Hebrews 11:6). Our walk as Christians is an ongoing journey of revelation leading to process, leading to more revelation and process. If this fails to occur, we'll probably make studying the Scriptures an end in itself and could one day find ourselves bushwhacked at a Bible study.

As powerful as the voice in the night was to me, it left me in a foggy, dreamlike state and lethargic to the task placed before me. But as usual, God is faithful, and in the next chapter I will share how He awakened me with a dream about a Green Ladder.

Questions to Ponder

1. Can you identify a paradigm shift in your own life that caused you to view the world or God completely differently?

2. How did this shift change your life?

3. Was this shift a *suddenly* or a slow process?

CHAPTER 2

THE GREEN LADDER DREAM

Three months passed after I was awakened by the voice in the night. I shared the story of that night with several of my friends, but my response to what I had heard was a big zero. However, God didn't wake me up so I could share a story about Him waking me up. He woke me up so I would write a book. Oh, I pondered it and prayed about it, and I was even preaching about the book on Sundays at church, but I just couldn't sit down and write. Something seemed to be missing, and I had no idea what that something was. I've had these feelings many times before in my life, and I knew what had to be done. I simply closed my eyes and prayed, *"Help."*

Pushed On by a Dream

That night the Lord gave me a very short and vivid dream that seemed to be the missing piece I was looking for. In this dream, I was a servant in a large estate house. During the course of my daily chores, the lady of the house called me in to speak with her. She told me she needed to use the ladder stored in the shed, and she wanted me to fix it up and get it ready for her. As the dream changed to the next scene, I found myself inside the shed staring at the ladder. At first, I couldn't figure out why she wanted this old thing fixed up at all, and I asked her to consider getting a new one. Her silent response said it all—as a servant I was simply to do what I had been told.

In the dream, the ladder before me was just a small stepladder with only three steps on it and was completely covered with a very hard, baked-on mud. Though I guessed the ladder was probably rotting underneath all the mud, it actually turned out to be surprisingly sturdy as I picked it up and examined it more closely. All I needed to do was remove the caked-on mud that was clinging to it, and my job would be done. The first thought that came to me was to simply scrape off the mud with a metal tool. After all, metal was harder than mud, and the mud should have easily given way. So I scraped and scraped and scraped with the metal tool, but I seemed to make very little progress for all the effort put forth. Then I had an idea: hose down the ladder with water to see if it would soften the hardened mud until it just washed off. To my complete surprise, this method worked wonders, and in a short period of time a beautiful green ladder with three steps was standing before me.

As soon as I awoke, I knew the dream had the fingerprints of God all over it, and I asked Him to explain it to me. The overall dream seemed to be broken up into three parts. In the first part of the dream, the large estate house symbolized the house of the Lord, and I was symbolically serving in this house. The lady of the house represented the Church, and she requested that I retrieve an old ladder that hadn't been used in years. The message seemed simple and straightforward to me—I was tasked with restoring the ladder and bringing it to the lady of the house because she needed it.

The second part of the dream seemed to highlight the natural wisdom of man in several ways. Once when I evaluated the old ladder, considered it worthless, and even recommended a new one. Then I used the logical choice of the metal tool to remove the caked-on mud.

We frequently read in the Scriptures that the ways of the Lord are not our ways. We often come up with newfangled plans and ways of doing things, and the Lord keeps pointing us back to the simple ways revealed in His Word. He didn't

> *The Lord keeps pointing us back to the simple ways revealed in His word.*
> ~

want me to build a new ladder. He wanted me to restore the old one. The metal tool wasn't an evil tool. It just wasn't the tool He had in mind for the task. In the dream, I worked especially hard with the metal tool and made very little progress for all the effort put out. In much the same way, God wants the Church to work smarter and not harder, and smarter implies hearing His voice and obeying it.

The last part of the dream was where I began to align myself with the Spirit and wisdom of God to accomplish the task placed before me. At first, hosing down the ladder with water seemed too foolish and easy, so I didn't even consider it. But then, after failing miserably with the metal tool, the foolish things of God seemed to make perfect sense to me. The water flowing from the hose symbolized the Word and the Spirit. When these two were joined together, they had all the power necessary to remove the old caked-on mud and to restore the ladder to its intended state. The metal tool would have worked fine for dried-on mud, but this mud needed the tools of the Spirit to remove it. The green of the ladder spoke to me of life, much as the evergreen trees of Oregon do. I sensed that the green in the dream wasn't just a color. It was far more than that. The Green Ladder seemed to radiate life, as if it was actually alive and growing. The Lord brought me back to the voice in the night and restated that the three steps were the three paradigm shifts He asked me to write about.

The only thing that puzzled me about the ladder was why it was so short. Something in me wanted the ladder of *Home Improvement's* Tim the Toolman—the Binford 5000—a huge, awesome, and overwhelming ladder reaching into the heavens. The response that came into my spirit was simply, *"You only need a small ladder, for the Kingdom of God is just a hand's length away."*

After putting together the voice in the night and the dream like pieces in a puzzle, my mission seemed much clearer to me—to write a book that would help bring about the restoration of three spiritual truths to the Church in

> *The kingdom of God is just a hand's length away.*
> ~

this crucial hour. Each chapter will contain Scriptures, stories, supernatural encounters, and illustrations that will remove the caked-on, religious mud that has put the Green Ladder out of service. The book is split into three additional sections, one for each step of the ladder. The first step identifies the gospel of the kingdom, the second reaffirms our identity in Christ, and the third illustrates the church co-laboring with a sovereign God to bring about *"on earth as it is in heaven"* (Matthew 6:10 NIV).

Before we go on with the story of the Green Ladder, we will need to take a small detour in the next chapter and speak about restoration; you can only restore something that has been lost or altered from its original state.

Questions to Ponder

1. Have you ever used the wrong tool for a work God called you to?

2. What was the outcome of using the wrong tool, and what did you learn from that?

3. Has God ever spoken to you in a dream and told you to do something?

CHAPTER 3

AS IT WAS IN THE BEGINNING

There's no doubt about it; our God is a restorer, and over and over again the prophets proclaimed His word to the nations, *"I will restore..."* The Random House Dictionary defines *restore* this way: *"a return of something to a former, original, normal or unimpaired condition; a restitution of something taken away or lost."* As I pondered the three steps of the Green Ladder more carefully, I began to see that God's plan for mankind has all three paradigms intact. In the opening chapters of Genesis, we find the following key phrases:

> *Let us make man in our image, in our likeness* [identity]...*the Lord God took the man and put him in the Garden of Eden to work it and take care of it* [co-laboring]...*be fruitful... multiply...fill the earth...subdue it...and rule* [co-laboring and advancing the rule of God as His delegated authorities] (Genesis 1:26; 2:15; 1:28 brackets added).

God placed a sense of identity, purpose, and destiny in

humanity at creation. God planted a garden in a place called Eden and placed the man He had created in it. Being created in the image and likeness of God enabled Adam to have face-to-face fellowship with his loving Father. In that place of intimacy, Adam's identity was firmly established, not because of what he would accomplish, but because of *whose he was*. He was the son of the Living God. As Adam's family increased, they were to subdue more and more of the earth, thus enlarging the borders of the garden and the kingdom of God in the earth. This is the co-mission that the Lord gave Adam and Eve in the beginning and with it came the power and authority to accomplish the task.

The Subduers Become the Subdued

Though God's original intent for Adam and Eve was to move them from a place of intimacy and identity to fulfill the commission given to them, this was no easy task. There was still the *subdue* part with which neither of them had any previous experience. At this point, the serpent entered the picture with a cunningness Adam and Eve had never encountered before, and they soon found their identity under attack. Though the serpent had no real power or authority to wield over Adam and Eve, he approached them with a weapon that neither of them was accustomed to—the weapon of words. In his craftiness, the serpent soon dislodged Eve from her rightful place with his subtleties and led her to reason on her own apart from the Word of God. As the assault continued, Eve finally came into agreement with him and ate the forbidden fruit. Then she influenced Adam with the serpent's logic, which tragically led to the Fall of the human race.

There's a Tad More to the Fall than a Fall

I'm not really sure why theologians call the incident in the

Garden the "Fall," because there seems to be a little more to it than that. A fall means you somehow tripped and stumbled, and all you need to do is get back up again. But after two thousand years of Patriarchs and another two thousand years of the Law and the Prophets, no one seemed to get back up again. Even adding a capital "F" on the word, implying a "Great Fall," doesn't adequately portray what happened in the Garden that day. As soon as Adam and Eve came into agreement with the serpent, they empowered him and gave him authority over their lives. Paul puts it this way:

> Don't you know that when you offer yourselves to someone to obey him as slaves, you are slaves to the one whom you obey—whether you are slaves to sin, which leads to death, or to obedience, which leads to righteousness?
> (Romans 6:16 NIV)

Adam and Eve offered themselves to the enemy by first listening to him and then finally obeying him. By their actions, Adam and Eve actually traded lords in the Garden that day and ushered the existence of the kingdom of darkness into the affairs of humankind.

What humanity needs is a King!

This is our problem, and simply trying to "get up" from the Fall isn't the solution. What humanity needs, plain and simple, is a King, and that's exactly what God in His infinite love and wisdom offers us in the gospel and the coming of Jesus.

God Makes a Prophetic Declaration

Right in the middle of this transaction in the Garden, God comes along and makes a prophetic declaration to Adam, Eve, and the serpent. God proclaimed that a Seed was coming—Jesus—and promised that what was lost would one day be redeemed and restored.

> *And I will put enmity between you and the woman, And between your seed and her Seed; He shall bruise your head, And you shall bruise His heel* (Genesis 3:15 NKJV).

Though the fulfillment of these words took thousands of years to come to pass, the promise remained true, and the promised seed finally came in the person of Jesus. As each of us comes to believe in Jesus, the rightful King and second man (this will be covered later in the book), we find ourselves placed in Him as new creations. In Him, the long dormant seeds that were stolen from Adam begin to come to life once again, and the original plan of God for humankind continues.

In the remainder of this book, we will discover together how the full atoning work of Jesus did far more than simply "pick up" the fallen human race. Step-by-step we will restore three heavenly paradigms to the Church as we discover our true identity in Christ as children of God who are to co-labor with Him and expand His kingdom on the earth.

So, let's go on to the first step of the Ladder.

Questions to Ponder

1. Can you remember a time when, like Eve, you reasoned from your intellect instead of the Word of God?

2. What was the outcome, and what did you learn from your experience?

3. Have you felt in your spirit what God was actually trying to restore in your life that was lost to mankind in the garden?

STEP ONE

THE GOSPEL OF THE KINGDOM

CHAPTER 4

THE SEED OF THE KINGDOM IS PLANTED

I began to experience the first paradigm shift back in 1982. For quite some time I had been in a spiritual holding pattern but was sensing that change was in the air. God was stirring a fresh hunger and expectancy among His people, and He had heard their cries. Something was coming. A shift was about to take place.

Born again as a hippie during the swell of the Jesus Movement in 1970, I was then caught up in the following wave of the Charismatic Renewal until it leveled out. Though it seemed calm in the wake of the Charismatic Renewal, I knew another wave was forming and prayed that I would not only be able to recognize the wave, but catch it as well.

Just Like a Vineyard

For the most part, it seemed like just another worship service in our little rural church on that Sunday morning in 1982. His presence was strong and sweet as we entered worship, and His Word and Spirit ministered life to the hearts in the room. But something was a little different that day. Near the front of the church were seven or eight visitors that just sat there and cried through most of the service, and I was curious as to why. When the meeting was finally over and everyone had greeted each other, I made my way over to them and asked them how they were doing. Though I expected to hear of some tragedy or loss of a loved one, I wasn't quite prepared for what came out of one of their mouths.

"This is just like a Vineyard," one of them said.

"A Vineyard," I said. *"What's that?"*

For the next hour they proceeded to tell me stories of a man named John Wimber and the Vineyard movement he started. Their accounts seemed to come right out of the Gospels and the book of Acts, where the Word of God was backed up by the works of God. I was used to having people come back from conferences and tell me what the speakers discussed, but these reports were more than that. These were about people getting healed and demons being cast out, manifestations and gifts of the Spirit flowing freely, and John Wimber telling people that everyone could suit up and play in the game. Everybody was capable of *"doin' the stuff,"* as John called it.

> *Their accounts seemed to come right out of the Gospels.*

By now my mind was racing and trying to process what I had just heard. Our church was similar to the Vineyard in many ways. We were a worshipping church, our dress was very casual, and my teaching style has always been transparent, but these people were describing something beyond our church culture. Could the stories they shared be true or was this some kind of false prophet or cult figure arising to deceive the Church with counterfeit miracles, signs, and wonders? Though my theology allowed for all of this, I personally wasn't seeing it happen on a regular basis and that troubled me. Sure, every now and then I saw what I've come to call an accidental healing, but that's exactly what it felt like—an accident.

Questions kept running through my mind, and I felt myself being divided into two different people. A part of me wanted to defend what I was currently experiencing in the realm of the Spirit and the supernatural, which was almost nothing. Another part of me was hoping all the stories were true and that I could still be taught how to "do the stuff" they were talking about.

The Scriptures certainly spoke enough about the disciples healing the sick and casting out demons and even said these kinds of signs would follow those who believe. But wait a minute—didn't I believe? By then I was spinning inside and wondering why a part of me would even want to defend my lack of supernatural experiences such as healing and deliverance. These newfound friends weren't arguing doctrines and theologies with me; they were recounting testimonies of the supernatural happenings they had personally observed and experienced. The Spirit of God had come in power. They had witnessed it personally, and now they were sharing their testimonies with me. Come to think of it, these were the very kind of stories that had helped bring me to Christ many years ago. *What could be simpler?* I thought to myself as I wondered if I had traded in *"having testimonies"* for *"having an argument."*

As mentioned earlier in the first chapter, paradigm shifts are essential, but not easy to embrace; they rarely come by having rational dialog and almost never come by having an argument. (Parents of teenagers understand this perfectly.) These shifts usually come to us by revelation and experience as the Lord moves in our lives, and are necessary for the transformation that conforms us into the image of His Son. So as great as the stories were, I knew I needed more information to settle the issues that were churning in my heart.

Come and See

As these new friends continued to talk, I believe they began to sense some of the inner conflicts and struggles I was having with God's supernatural power, struggles they had probably worked through in their own lives. It was here that the conversation slowly came to a close, and they told me that they were going to see John Wimber up in the Seattle area and asked if I would like to go with them. As soon as the question was asked, there was an immediate response in my spirit, and I heard three simple words ring out inside of me: *come and see.*

Days later, I was in Seattle gearing up for my first encounter with John Wimber. Personally and pastorally I felt I needed to know more about this man and his message that was stirring up the body of Christ. I wondered if he was bringing some strange twisted doctrine from an obscure passage in Ezekiel, or if he was given a message from God that would birth a movement like Martin Luther or John Wesley, who were received by some and cursed by others. My plan was to go to the meetings with an open mind and to process it later, like one of the noble Bereans mentioned in Acts 17 who searched the Scriptures to see if what they had heard Paul say was true. I would be at a pastor's conference in the mornings and afternoons with about 300 other pastors and at a healing seminar in the evenings that was open to the public.

"I came, I saw, I got blowed up!"
—Ernest Goes to Jail

This conference was absolutely life changing. (When I walked in the door of our home after the conference, my wife actually asked me, *"What happened to you?"*)

Being with John Wimber was an amazing experience. He was unlike anyone I had ever encountered. He was "real." Though he described himself as simply *"a fat man trying to get to Heaven,"* he was much more than that. He was the first person I had ever met who resembled Jesus' disciples in their display of supernatural phenomena. He was a student, open to risk and failure, and always pressing into more of God. He was full of love, mercy, and kindness and had an incredible twinkle in his eye, and was secure enough in God to laugh about himself. He was willing to be a fool for Christ, but his radical faith was contagious. In a time when there were ten thousand teachers, he arose as a father, a father that wanted to freely give away all that God had given him, so those who would receive could go beyond him.

> *He believed in "equipping the saints to do the works of the ministry."*
> ∼

So what did I see and hear for the next three days? I saw the love of God demonstrated in power. I saw more healings in a single meeting than I had seen since becoming a Christian twelve years earlier. I saw people delivered from demons (I thought they were all in Africa) and even witnessed a creative miracle of a toe growing out that had been cut off by a lawnmower.

The amazing thing about these meetings is that the miracles mentioned above weren't done by John Wimber but by the people participating at the conference. He believed in *"equipping the saints to do the works of the ministry"* (see Ephesians 4:12), and that's exactly what happened. We all got to suit up and play. I now had stories of my own about what I had seen and heard that I could share with others.

But what exactly did John Wimber do that caused that first paradigm shift in my life that would alter me forever? I simply heard him share the gospel—the gospel of the kingdom. There was no obscure text drawn from Ezekiel, just familiar passages from the Gospels I'd read over and over—but had been unable to see and hear because I was looking through the preconceived lens of the gospel of salvation. John's messages on the gospel of the kingdom were simple and full of Scriptures, and were confirmed with signs and wonders just as the messages of the early disciples had been. In Matthew 13, Jesus taught the parable of the sower and shared that the farmer sowed "the message of the kingdom" into the hearts of people. That's what I felt happened to me that weekend in Seattle, and it was now my job to protect and nurture the seed that was sown into my heart so that it could bring forth kingdom fruit.

Here are two verses from First Corinthians that kept running through my mind on the long drive home from the conference:

> *My message and my preaching were not with wise and persuasive words, but with a demonstration of the Spirit's power, so that your faith might not rest on men's wisdom, but on God's power* (1 Corinthians 2:4-5 NIV).

> *For the kingdom of God is not a matter of talk but of power* (1 Corinthians 4:20 NIV).

Let's go see what this gospel of the kingdom is and how

it's meant to bring about a radical shift in our thinking and actions.

Questions to Ponder

1. When have you experienced the difference between "having a testimony" and "having an argument"?

2. How have you experienced the Word of God turning into the Works of God?

3. How do you protect and nurture the seed of the Word that's been sown into your heart?

CHAPTER 5

SHIFTING TO THE GOSPEL OF THE KINGDOM

One of the hardest parts of having a paradigm shift is learning how to process what you once held as true with what you're currently holding as true. Do we get angry about the paradigms we held yesterday, or do we see them as transitions to what we're experiencing today? And do we even consider the possibility that what we've come to embrace as true today may go through another paradigm shift in the future? This all gets further complicated when we want to share the newfound truths we have received with others.

This is something all of us experienced when we came to Christ. What was true yesterday is no longer true today. It's easy to sing, *"I once was lost, but now I'm found, was blind but now I see,"* when yesterday we wouldn't have said we were either lost or blind. As many of us tried to share this good news with others, we were actually shocked that they couldn't *see* they were lost or blind. What was even more troubling was when they became concerned that we felt we were now found and could see.

Think of being a flat-world sailor who had just experienced a round-world paradigm shift. Do you think you would feel stupid for believing the world was flat or angry with those who had taught it to you? Or would you be able to process this, aware that even you didn't believe the round-world revelation the first time you heard it? Even though you were now confident that the world was round and you couldn't go over the edge, I suppose the next time you sailed off into the sunset your flat-world friends were there to warn and pray for you.

Up until I had encountered John Wimber's ministry, I had only heard and preached the gospel of salvation. The entire focus of my ministry was aimed at sharing the message of salvation with unbelievers in the hopes that they might receive Christ, thus securing their eternal security in heaven when they died. This is a great message, and I still preach it today. But it is not, however, a complete message, and it is not the full message that Jesus preached.

Jesus did not walk this earth only trying to get people saved. No, He said things like, "the kingdom of heaven is at hand." Jesus invited people into a relationship with the King and His kingdom and the doorway into that kingdom is

> Jesus was concerned with getting Heaven into People more than getting people into Heaven.

salvation. When people in Jesus' day encountered the kingdom, they were saved, healed, delivered, and empowered. Jesus was concerned with getting Heaven into people more than getting people into Heaven. The disciples walked in power and brought the kingdom wherever they went because the King (and His dominion) lived inside of them.

I had unknowingly reduced the gospel to a message of

salvation. I brought people into a relationship with the King, but I was not experiencing a full life in the kingdom characterized by signs, wonders, miracles, healings, and deliverances. I brought people through the door of salvation, but no one was experiencing the kingdom like the disciples did. When our entire focus is on getting people to Heaven, we miss that God wants to bring His kingdom and influence to earth in and through us.

During the Charismatic Renewal, millions of Christians encountered one of the greatest paradigm shifts of their Christianity. Moved by their hunger for God and hearing that *"there is more,"* they entered into the Baptism of the Holy Spirit, spoke in tongues, and began to exercise the gifts of the Spirit. When these Charismatics tried to share these new paradigms with their pastors and friends, they were often met with great resistance and warnings of being deceived by the devil.

The Lord spoke something to my heart many years ago that has helped me along this journey. He told me that I must be convinced of two things: that what I'm presently embracing is the truth, and what I'm presently embracing isn't all the truth. This statement opened me up to hear the accounts of my brothers and their victorious journeys into the Promised Land of new truth and to share in our corporate inheritance. Regardless of how much we've come to know God, there's always going to be more. No theological box can contain all of Him, and He has designed us to glean from those who have gone before us in the journey.

I don't consider myself a Catholic, a Lutheran, a Methodist, or a Pentecostal, but someone who honors the wealth in all these denominations and who gets to receive the inheritance they fought for and won in our Promised Land. I've personally dropped the labels of evangelical and Pentecostal simply because these labels, and the arguments they bring, can't be found in the Scriptures. When Paul asked the church at Ephesus if they had received the Holy Spirit when they believed, they didn't answer by telling him they were evangelicals. They simply told him they hadn't heard about the Holy Spirit yet (see Acts 19). Their answer allowed them to stay on a learning curve and remain open for more of what the Lord had for them. It's interesting to note that the church at Ephesus became one of the greatest churches in the New Testament and in history.

Jesus said He had many other things to tell His disciples but they wouldn't be able to handle them at that time. The Spirit would lead them into these things later on as they were able to understand them (see John 16:12). Though Jesus is the Truth, the Spirit is the guide that leads us deeper and deeper into Truth. There's always more. It's bigger than all of our boxes, doctrines, and theologies.

In all this, my personal philosophy is very simple; I am just trying to look and act like the boys in the Book. To do that I have had to break a lot of my boxes, re-examine my doctrines, and drop many of the labels that have been so divisive. It's actually quite refreshing to become a wide-eyed child again and simply walk with my loving Father, the Living God, and not have to have all the answers.

> *I'm just trying to look and act like the boys in the Book.*

I'm not here to argue with anyone, since I've discovered that God rarely anoints an argument. Moving from the gospel of salvation to the gospel of the kingdom was both hard and marvelous for me. I didn't plan it; I was led by the Spirit into it and did what many of you will do— took off my preconceived lenses and searched the Scriptures. I believed the message of salvation and had preached it for twelve years, and it was all good and great, but when the Lord opened my eyes to see the gospel of the kingdom, many of the questions and tensions I had were settled. So, come and see.

The Gospel According to Jesus

As ambassadors of Christ, we've been given a message to proclaim to the nations. This message is called the *gospel*, which simply means the *good news*. As His representatives on the earth, we need to be clear about the contents of this message because the wrong message will produce the wrong results. (The Scriptures give two warnings about receiving a different gospel. See 2 Corinthians 11:3-4; Galatians 1:6-7.) Consider reading the following Scriptures in a new light.

> *Now after John was put in prison, Jesus came to Galilee, preaching the **gospel of the kingdom** of God and saying, "The time is fulfilled, and the **kingdom of God is at hand**. Repent, and believe in the gospel"* (Mark 1:14-15 NKJV).

The first part of the verse is fairly simple; Jesus is preaching the *gospel of the kingdom* of God and not the *gospel of salvation*. Certainly the one who is called the Word could have used the term gospel of salvation if He wanted to. If He felt the gospel of salvation was interchangeable or synonymous with the gospel of the kingdom, He may have used it. But He didn't. God says what He means and means what He says. (After all my years in the Scriptures and in pastoral ministry, I have concluded that the Word of God is so simple that we need help to misunderstand it—and we've had lots of help.)

In the next phrase, Jesus tells us that *"the time is fulfilled, and the kingdom of God is at hand"* (Mark 1:15). Everything is now ready for what was prophesied in the Garden and promised to

Abraham, foretold by the Prophets and foreshadowed in the Law. The rightful King (though not yet recognized) has come and He's brought His kingdom (His rule, reign, and dominion) with Him. This kingdom isn't far away or futuristic; it's here and now and it's close at hand; in fact, it's just a hand's reach away. Two verses will help to shed some light for us here:

> *But the angel said to them, "Do not be afraid. I bring you good news of great joy that will be for all the people. Today in the town of David a Savior has been born to you; he is Christ the Lord* (Luke 2:10-11 NIV).

> *"You are a king, then!" said Pilate.*

> *Jesus answered, "You are right in saying I am a king. In fact, for this reason I was born, and for this I came into the world, to testify to the truth. Everyone on the side of truth listens to me"* (John 18:37 NIV).

In the first verse, the angel shares that the good news is that a Savior has been born and that Savior is Christ the Lord. Christ isn't the last name of Jesus. It's the Greek rendering for the Hebrew word Messiah. However you view the contents of the Old Testament, this Messiah, or Anointed One, was to be the King that would usher in the kingdom.

In the second verse, Jesus tells Pilate straight out that He was born to be king. Put simply, the Messiah or King has come and He will save you. The King is the Savior. We've all heard teachings with phrases like, "*You've made*

> *The King saves you because the King **is** the Savior and Lord.*
>

Him your Savior, and now it's time to make Him your Lord and King." These teachings usually flow out of our understanding of the gospel of salvation. But with the gospel of the kingdom, the King saves you because the King *is* the Savior and Lord.

The final phrase of Jesus, "*Repent, and believe in the gospel,*" totally reinforces the concept of the gospel of the kingdom. Our trouble usually lies with the word "repent," and our limited understanding of its meaning. It certainly includes the usual remorse and confession of sins, but the word also means to change your mind and the way you think. When Jesus spoke this word to the multitudes, there was no Calvary, no cross, and no bloodshed yet. Because of our gospel-of-salvation lens, we automatically put all that into the word repent, but the text doesn't support that unless the gospel mentioned is the gospel of salvation.

But, as we've already seen, Jesus came and preached the gospel of the kingdom of God. Jesus wasn't telling them to repent and confess their sins. He was telling them to repent and change the way they had been thinking about the kingdom of God. Believe it or not, Jesus, the rightful and true King, invaded this dark planet at His incarnation, and He established a stronghold from which to advance His kingdom. (A little later we will see how Jesus' announcement was actually a declaration of war and proclaimed the clash of the kingdoms.)

Our Salvation is in the Gospel of the Kingdom

You may be tempted to think I'm doing away with the great theme of salvation. Let me assure you I'm not. Our salvation is neatly enveloped within the gospel of the kingdom that Jesus proclaimed. God's idea of salvation isn't only God loving and forgiving, but God ruling and reigning.

Let me play around for a moment with some of the various

gospel messages we often hear. If someone were unfamiliar with the gospel message and was told it was love, or forgiveness, or eternal life, it would only be part of the whole gospel truth. Each part, though, would be contained within the gospel of the kingdom. Suppose I'm a heroin addict and I hear that the gospel is that Jesus loves me. Great! Now I'm a loved heroin addict. But then I hear that God loves me and sent His son to die for me so that my sins could be forgiven. This is a little better for now I'm a loved and forgiven heroin addict. The next message I hear is that God has good news for me, and I can live with Him forever in Heaven. This message just gets better and better. Now I'm a loved and forgiven heroin addict that gets to spend eternity with God in Heaven. Please understand, I love all the benefits of the various gospel messages and understand the biblical base for all of them. But these are really all a part of the gospel of the Kingdom. Where He rules, His love and forgiveness freely flow. Where His power and authority are demonstrated, demonic powers of addictions and death are done away with.

The Gospel of the Kingdom in the Middle and End of Jesus' Ministry

> *After this, Jesus traveled about from one town and village to another, proclaiming the good news of the kingdom of God* (Luke 8:1 NIV).

> *But the crowds learned about it and followed him. He welcomed them and spoke to them about the kingdom of God, and healed those who needed healing* (Luke 9:11 NIV).

From these texts we are assured that Jesus started preaching the message of the kingdom of God and continued to do so in the middle of His ministry. But what about after He suffered on the cross, shed His blood, and rose from the grave? Did His message change from the kingdom of God to something else? Let's see.

> *After his suffering, he showed himself to these*
> *men and gave many convincing proofs that he*
> *was alive. He appeared to them over a period*
> *of forty days and spoke about the* **kingdom of**
> **God** (Acts 1:3 NIV).

Did you catch that? Jesus was getting ready to pass the baton to His disciples and wanted to make sure they really understood the message clearly. So off and on for forty days He spoke about one thing and one thing only: the kingdom of God. Jesus was a kingdom man through and through. After all, He's the King. He demonstrated it, sought it first, and then taught us also to pray, *"Your Kingdom come" until "the kingdoms of this world have become the Kingdoms of our Lord and of His Christ"* (see Matthew 6:10; Revelation 11:15).

Even though we have only looked at a couple of verses in the gospels, it's clear that the message Jesus proclaimed was the gospel of the kingdom of God and not the gospel of salvation. These aren't rare and isolated verses; the kingdom of God is mentioned in the gospels just as many times as the word *love*, over 58 times.

The Most Important Paradigm Shift of All: Stepping into the New Covenant

The scope of this book mainly deals with paradigm shifts within the New Testament. I felt, however, that before I ended this chapter I should quote one significant verse dealing with a major shift between the Old and New Testaments. Jesus came to lead us into the greatest paradigm shift of all—out of the law and performance and into the grace and relationship of the new covenant. He then went on to institute the new covenant, making the old covenant and all its demands obsolete (see Hebrews 8:13).

On the same night He gave them the new covenant, He also gave them the new command—to *"love each other as I have loved you"* (see John 13:34; 15:12,17).

Let's move on and see if the disciples preached the same message.

Questions to Ponder

1. How do you stay open and hungry for the next truth God wants to bring you?

2. What boxes, doctrines or labels have you left behind in order to go forward in God?

3. What do you understand about the gospel of the Kingdom? How is it different from the gospel of Salvation?

CHAPTER 6

THE MESSAGE OF THE KINGDOM PASSED ON

One of the party games I played as a child, "Telephone," has come to mind many times through the years. In this game a large group of people form a circle and the leader tells the person next to him or her a story. This next person then tells the next person until the story is passed around the circle and comes back to the leader. I thought it was a silly game, at first, until I heard how far the story had deviated from the original, and wondered how it happened. As a pastor, I have witnessed similar phenomena several times over the years as simple stories turned into comedies or tragedies before my eyes.

In 1984, for example, a strong wave of healing and deliverance hit our little church, and people visited from all over southern Oregon. On one occasion, a lady who had heard some of these accounts came to a few members of our staff for ministry. After spending a brief time interviewing her, we stood and told her it was time to pray. All of a sudden a look of fear came over her face. We asked her what was wrong. She told us that she had heard we used pillows and sticks when we had ministry time. What? Where did that come from? (What shocked us the most wasn't that she heard the stories of us using pillows and sticks, but that she had come for a time of prayer anyway!) We quickly assured her that we didn't minister to people using pillows and sticks. We laugh about it now, but at the time we were genuinely puzzled about how testimonies of our ministry had evolved into such interesting tales.

Though I'm not exactly sure where it was in church history that the story of the gospel of the kingdom transitioned into the gospel of salvation, I don't believe it was the result of a malicious plot. It was probably a slow and subtle change that took decades to become the acceptable norm in the Church. Fortunately for the Church, the Lord has given us His Word and Spirit to awaken us during times of transition and restoration. So let's continue looking into the Scripture to see the message that was passed on to the disciples and the early church.

The Message of the Kingdom of God to the Twelve Disciples

> When Jesus had called the Twelve together, he gave them power and authority to drive out all demons and to cure diseases, and he sent them out to preach the kingdom of God and to heal the sick (Luke 9:1-2 NIV).

From the text it is clear that these first disciples had the same message and mandate as their Master—the message of the kingdom of God. Though we will pick this thought up at a later time, notice that the **words** of the kingdom were also coupled with the **works** of the kingdom. As modeled to the disciples by Jesus, the proclamation of the good news was to be followed with a demonstration—God confirming His Word with signs and wonders.

The Seventy Preach the Kingdom

> Heal the sick who are there and tell them, "The kingdom of God is near you" (Luke 10:9 NIV).

Here again we find Jesus giving the same message to the seventy that He had given to the twelve disciples: the message of the kingdom of God. It's also clear from the text that He not only delivered the message of the kingdom to them, but also gave them power and authority to demonstrate that the King was indeed close at hand and confirming His Word with signs and wonders.

The Apostle Paul Proclaims the Kingdom

Since Paul is the author of most of the New Testament writings, it's crucial that we look closely at the message he preached during the days of the early church. Was there a different word proclaimed after Jesus shed His blood at Calvary, rose from the dead, ascended into the heavens, and poured out the Holy Spirit on the Church? Or was it the same directive that Jesus preached years earlier—the message of the kingdom of God?

What is encouraging to me about the Apostle Paul is that, according to the Scriptures, he never knew the physical Jesus of the gospels. What Paul received, he received from the Holy Spirit, who is the same teacher that is available to all of us today. Jesus is indeed the Truth, but the

> *The Spirit of Truth leads and guides us into the truth of Jesus.*
> ∼

Holy Spirit is the Spirit of Truth that leads and guides us into the truth of Jesus. So let's look at the words the Spirit brought to this prominent servant of the early church.

> *Paul entered the synagogue and spoke boldly there for three months, arguing persuasively about **the kingdom of God*** (Acts 19:8 NIV).

> *Now I know that none of you among whom I have gone about **preaching the kingdom** will ever see me again* (Acts 20:25 NIV).

> *They arranged to meet Paul on a certain day, and came in even larger numbers to the place where he was staying. From morning till evening he explained and declared to them the **kingdom of God** and tried to convince them about Jesus from the Law of Moses and from the Prophets* (Acts 28:23 NIV).

> *Boldly and without hindrance **he preached the kingdom of God** and taught about the Lord Jesus Christ* (Acts 28:31 NIV).

From these Scriptures it is evident that Paul carried the message of the kingdom of God to the nations. In him, God had found a zealous and brilliant man who was knowledgeable in the Scriptures, and added to him the power, authority, and revelations of the Holy Spirit to create a leader who helped turn the known world upside down. The last sentence of the book of Acts says it so well: *he preached the kingdom of God and taught about the Lord Jesus Christ* (Acts 28:31). Paul spent his time talking about the King and His kingdom.

Philip, a Post-Resurrection Disciple

Philip is another great example of a disciple in the book of Acts who was filled with the Spirit and preached the message of the kingdom of God with signs and wonders following.

> *Philip went down to a city in Samaria and proclaimed the Christ there. When the crowds heard Philip and saw the miraculous signs he did, they all paid close attention to what he said. With shrieks, evil spirits came out of many, and many paralytics and cripples were healed. So there was great joy in that city* (Acts 8:5-8 NIV).

> *But when they believed Philip as he preached the good news of the* **kingdom of God** *and the name of Jesus Christ, they were baptized, both men and women. Simon himself believed and was baptized. And he followed Philip everywhere, astonished by the great signs and miracles he saw* (Acts 8:12-13 NIV).

The Gospel of the Kingdom to the End

It's necessary for the gospel of the kingdom to be the first step restored on the Green Ladder. When the message of Jesus becomes the message of the Church, we will finally discover our true destiny and identity in Him. This is the paradigm shift that changes the focus of the Church from *going to Heaven* to *bringing Heaven down to the earth.* Jesus ascended into Heaven and poured out the Holy Spirit. He passed the baton to His disciples, the commissioned ones sent by the King to advance the kingdom of God into the earth. This shift to the gospel of the kingdom is going on all over the world. Signs, wonders, and miracles are exploding and great harvests are seen in the wake of the proclamation of the good news—the King has come and He has brought His kingdom with Him. The gospel Jesus preached and passed on to His disciples has never changed and is to be proclaimed by us until the very end, until *the kingdoms of this world have become the kingdoms of our Lord and of His Christ* (see Revelation 11:15).

> *And this gospel of the kingdom will be preached in the whole world as a testimony to all nations, and then the end will come* (Matthew 24:14 NIV).

In the next chapter we'll see how the message of the kingdom of God has the ability to bring your life into simple focus.

Questions to Ponder

1. How have you shifted from just wanting to go to Heaven to wanting to bring Heaven down to earth?

2. Has this shift changed how you think and what you do?

3. What has helped you process shifting from the gospel of salvation to the gospel of the kingdom?

Chapter 7

Seek First the Kingdom of God

After six years of pastoring a church in Grants Pass, Oregon, I began to feel a little tired and worn out. Though I had a heart for pastoring and really loved it, I seemed to be spinning my wheels more and advancing less. I felt as if I was chasing the wind instead of being caught up by the wind, and a slow weariness and frustration came over me.

The church growth movement was on the rise in America, and I was slowly losing my joy as I diligently applied the techniques and labored to build my church. All of this felt awkward to me, like Saul's armor on David. But I didn't know what else to do. Most of my energy was spent on putting out various fires that popped up in the lives of the people and the fellowship. I'd get the call, hear the problem, and run out with my bucket of water. Though the people were happy with my attention focused on them and the problems in the church, I just felt out of step. The strange thing was that church attendance was actually increasing during this time, but I felt I was creating a pile of bricks rather than a habitation for the Lord. I was tired, weary, frustrated, and successful when His gentle voice came to me and said, *"I didn't call you to put out brush fires, I called you to plant a forest."*

What follows are some of the key verses that the Lord illuminated to me during this time that restored the first step of the Green Ladder—the gospel of the kingdom—in my life and in our fellowship.

The All-Encompassing Kingdom

The Gospel of the kingdom isn't just the message we speak; it's the life we live. It's to be the entire focal point of our lives and everything our lives contain. Nothing is to be considered too small or insignificant. Simply put, the kingdom of God is where the rule and reign of the King has come, and it's always advancing and increasing in us, through us, and around us. It's the bull's eye on the target we are continually aiming for, and when we hit it, it has the rippling effect of a rock thrown into a pond that reaches everything beyond it.

In Matthew 6, we find Jesus teaching people who were deprived of the basic necessities of life by an evil king. Jesus encouraged them to seek first the rule and reign of a good king and his kingdom—God and His kingdom.

> *Therefore do not worry, saying, "What shall we eat?" or "What shall we drink?" or "What shall we wear?" For after all these things the Gentiles seek. For your heavenly Father knows that you need all these things. But seek first the kingdom of God and His righteousness, and all these things shall be added to you* (Matthew 6:31-33 NKJV).

As we seek the rule and reign of the kingdom of God first, all other things begin to fall into place. For many of us, this seems odd because we usually view kings and kingdoms as evil. Hollywood depicts evil monarchies that need to be dethroned so democracy can be put in its place. But God is a good and loving King, a heavenly Father. He invites us to come into His family and under His rulership where He can care for us, supply for us, and protect us.

"Seek first" brings a simple focus into our lives because all we have to do is keep the first things first. What really makes this easy is that there is no "seek second" in the Scriptures. We can never again say we don't know what the will of God is in a given situation. His will is His kingdom, and His kingdom is His will. Jesus and Heaven are our model. It doesn't matter if we're dealing with something physical or spiritual, mental or relational, or vocational or financial; our job is to simply seek first the kingdom of God.

The Kingdom is Relational

It is helpful to remind ourselves that the kingdom only exists because of the King. In our Western world, we tend to reduce the kingdom to understanding principles instead of relating to the person and presence of the King. Life has principles, but those principles don't necessarily bring life.

> *We tend to reduce the Kingdom to understanding principles instead of relating to the person and presence of the King.*

To illustrate, picture the face of a clock. Now replace all the numbers with a small dot and place a big dot in the middle of the face where the hands would be. Each of the outer dots could be labeled with anything pertaining to life— marriage, child rearing, finances, vocations—and the center dot would be marked as the kingdom of God. Instead

> *Life has principles, but principles have no life in themselves.*

of teaching on all the kingdom principles of the small, outer dots, what would happen if we just took the advice of Jesus to seek first the kingdom of God? If King Jesus ruled in our lives, our finances would begin to come into order not because of a kingdom principle, but because of a relationship with the King that involved seeking His face, hearing His voice, and obeying in faith. Jesus designed the kingdom of God to be advanced by our interaction and communion with the King Himself. The fruit of this relationship would be better marriages and parenting, ordered finances, constant miracles and healings, and so on. Let's listen to the warning Jesus gives in Matthew 7 to those who were advancing the kingdom without relating to the King.

> *Many will say to me on that day, "Lord, Lord, did we not prophesy in your name, and in your name drive out demons and perform many miracles?" Then I will tell them plainly, "I never knew you. Away from me, you evildoers!"* (Matthew 7:22-23 NIV)

Life has principles, but principles have no life in themselves. It is entirely possible for non-believers to embrace and reap the benefits of kingdom principles, like giving or tithing, and yet have no interaction with the King in any way. But without that interaction there will be no faith, and without faith it's impossible to please God, and that's what it's all about. As seen in the verse above, even those casting out demons and working miracles would hear Jesus tell them to go away because He never knew them. But why would He do that? Because at the center of the gospel is relationship with the King and they didn't have one.

Kingdom Prayer

Jesus also taught that the kingdom of God was to be the focal point of our prayers and intercession. Though there are many different types of prayers mentioned in the Bible, and all are good in their proper place, Jesus taught the disciples to pray kingdom prayers—prayers that invite Heaven to manifest on the earth.

> This, then, is how you should pray: "Our Father in heaven, hallowed be your name, your kingdom come, your will be done on earth as it is in heaven" (Matthew 6:9-10 NIV).

The *message* of the kingdom is connected to the *power* of the kingdom by the *prayers* of the kingdom. Jesus modeled this and encouraged His disciples to do the same. (This concept will be covered more thoroughly in the third section of the book.)

The Kingdom Is in the Realm of the Spirit

One of the hardest aspects of the kingdom of God for us Westerners to understand is that the kingdom flows from the unseen realm of the Spirit. Our strong empirical worldview has subtly removed us from the things that are unseen and supernatural, and caused us to align ourselves unknowingly with the spirit of antichrist. Notice that the term is anti-Christ and not anti-Jesus. Christ is the Greek word used for Messiah, which means *anointed* or *anointed one; the one anointed by God and empowered by God's Spirit to deliver His people and establish His kingdom.* Though we usually use this term to refer to some evil boogeyman coming in the future (and I'm not saying it isn't), antichrist is anti-anointing, anti-empowering, and anti-supernatural. The antichrist spirit is suspicious of signs, wonders, healings, and miracles.

In fact, the Sadducees, part of the religious ruling class in the days of Jesus, didn't believe in angels, spirits, or the resurrection. In his first letter, John used antichrist to describe those that didn't believe in

> *It is possible to love the Jesus of the gospels and to be resistant to the realm of the supernatural.*

the incarnation. It is possible to love the Jesus of the gospels and the miracles He did, but to be resistant to the realm of the supernatural. We often agree theologically with the concepts of signs and wonders, miracles and healings, and angels and demons manifesting, but these supernatural phenomena rarely, if ever, show up in our practices.

Though Jesus was born as King in a manger, it wasn't until after the Holy Spirit came upon Him at His baptism that we begin to see His kingdom advance into the earth.

> *But if I drive out demons by the Spirit of God,*
> *then the kingdom of God has come upon you*
> (Matthew 12:28 NIV).

In the above verse, we see that the kingdom of God was advanced as Jesus drove out demons by the power of the Holy Spirit and not because He was God. Jesus laid aside His divinity and His equality with God at the incarnation and operated as a man who was in right relationship with God and anointed with the Holy Spirit. This is great news for all believers and is part of the paradigm shift that takes place as we embrace the gospel of the kingdom. Jesus is the prototype for all who would believe and follow Him. He modeled for all of us what it looks like to be born of the Spirit and empowered by the Spirit as He advanced the kingdom of God through the Spirit. In fact, any advancement of the kingdom is because of the Spirit, since the kingdom of God is in the realm of the Holy Spirit. Whether the kingdom is coming to us or flowing through us, it all originates from the unseen realm of the Spirit and being made manifest in the earth.

> *For the kingdom of God is not a matter of eating and drinking, but of righteousness, peace and joy in the Holy Spirit* (Romans 14:17 NIV).

The gospel of the kingdom was the centering point on the potter's wheel that totally captivated the life of Jesus. It's what He lived, prayed, and demonstrated to the world, and it's what He passed on to His disciples to declare until the end. In contrast to the gospel of salvation that focuses on getting people to Heaven, the gospel of the kingdom is involved with bringing the kingdom of God into the earth, first in and then through His disciples. This gospel sets forth the clash of the kingdoms of light and darkness that began when Jesus invaded the earth in His incarnation. When Jesus' disciples were filled with the Spirit on the day of Pentecost it established a beachhead. For us who believe and follow in the footsteps of our Lord, the battle goes on until *"the kingdoms of this world have become the kingdoms of our Lord and of His Christ, and He shall reign forever and ever!"* (Revelation 11:15).

Let's move on to the next step of the Green Ladder where we transition from having a sinner/shame-based identity to having a righteousness/saint-based identity.

Questions to Ponder

1. In what parts of your life have you experienced relating to the person and presence of the King?

2. How do you interact and commune with the King Himself?

3. How has "seeking first the kingdom of God" and praying for the "kingdom of God to come on earth as it is in Heaven" brought more focus into your life?

STEP 2

I'm a Saint, Not a Sinner!

CHAPTER 8

THE PEOPLE OF THE KINGDOM

Now both of your feet are firmly planted on the first step of the Green Ladder—the gospel of the kingdom of God. From here we are able to move onto the second step of the Ladder that deals with our new identity in Christ. We received it by responding to the gospel, putting our faith in Jesus, and becoming "born again." Whereas the first step of the Ladder gives us the message of the kingdom, the second step deals with the people of the kingdom and our new identity as sons and daughters of God.

Though the problem of identity theft seems to be a recent issue coming out of our technological age, it's actually been with us for thousands of years. In fact, the first identity theft took place in the Garden when Adam and Eve empowered the thief by believing the lies that he told them about themselves instead of what God had told them. The enemy knows that identity is crucial to the advancement of the kingdom of God and does everything in his power to keep us in the dark about our true identity in Jesus. Why? Because who we are, or should I say who we think we are, will determine what we'll do, and that's exactly what the enemy fears the most. He doesn't mind the church **believing**. He minds the church actually **doing**.

Though the New Testament speaks volumes to us concerning our new identity in Christ, there seems to be a spiritual amnesia over much of the church today. The main symptoms of this amnesia are that we've partially or completely forgotten:

1. Who we are

2. Where we've come from (who's our daddy?)

3. What we're supposed to be doing.

Looking at "Born Again" Again

In recent years the term *born again* has become very popular in Christian circles and beyond. As is often the case with phrases that spread out far and wide, they begin to lose their original meaning and impact. Because of this, it will be helpful to take a second look at the term *born again*. Preachers of the gospel of salvation often use the term to mean getting saved or getting right with God. They usually tie it in with having eternal life and going to heaven some day. But as we've already seen in our first paradigm shift, Jesus didn't come preaching the gospel of salvation. Rather, He preached the gospel of the kingdom of God. In order to understand this pivotal phrase more clearly, let's look to the Scriptures and see it within the context that Jesus first introduced it.

> *Now there was a man of the Pharisees named Nicodemus, a member of the Jewish ruling council. He came to Jesus at night and said, "Rabbi, we know you are a teacher who has come from God. For no one could perform the miraculous signs you are doing if God were not with him."*

In reply Jesus declared, "I tell you the truth,
no one can see the kingdom of God unless he
is born again."

"How can a man be born when he is old?"
Nicodemus asked. "Surely he cannot enter
a second time into his mother's womb to be
born!"

Jesus answered, "I tell you the truth, no one
can enter the kingdom of God unless he is
born of water and the Spirit. Flesh gives birth
to flesh, but the Spirit gives birth to spirit.
You should not be surprised at my saying,
'You must be born again'" (John 3:1-7 NIV).

Most of us have read and heard this passage preached many
times. After all, it's the classic text for talking about the incredible
event of being born again, and we all know *we must be born*
again. Unfortunately, we usually read this through a gospel-of-
salvation lens and miss some of the major points Jesus is trying
to make. The New Testament Scriptures declare that if one is
born again they would have their sins forgiven, eternal life, and a
home in Heaven. Jesus doesn't touch on any of those points in His
discourse with Nicodemus. So what is His point? It's really quite
simple when you read the story again through a kingdom-of-God
worldview.

In his world, Nicodemus would have been considered a very
religious, moral, and synagogue-going man. As a Pharisee, he
was well educated in the Scriptures, maintained the religious
traditions and customs passed down to him from the days of
Moses, and held tightly to the letter of the Law. He had obviously
heard Jesus proclaiming the good news of the kingdom of God
and had seen Him perform many miracles, signs, and wonders.

From what he had personally seen and heard concerning Jesus, Nicodemus came to the following conclusion—Jesus must be a teacher sent from God.

Though Nicodemus didn't specifically ask Jesus a question, Jesus responds to him as if he had. It's here that Jesus introduces us to the concept of being born again, and places this pivotal phrase in the very context of the kingdom of God. In His interaction with Nicodemus, Jesus gives him three main points to consider, two of which begin with the phrase, *"I tell you the truth."* In today's language Jesus is saying something like, "Listen-up real good now, Nick, 'cause I'm about to tell you something so awesome that it's going to blow your mind. In fact, it's going to sound too good to be true, but it is, Nick. It's really true."

Jesus begins by telling Nicodemus that he must be born again to see the kingdom of God. His second point builds on this as Jesus states that we must be born again to enter the kingdom of God. Did you catch that? We get to see and enter the kingdom of God *right now* as we become born again.

> *We get to see and enter the kingdom of God right now as we become born again.*
> ∽

Nicodemus then tells Jesus he's confused by this born-again language and wonders how he could get back into his mother's womb since he's now a grown man. Jesus responds to him with His third point and tells him that this birth isn't a natural birth from the flesh, but is actually a birth from the Spirit.

When we grasp what Jesus is sharing with Nicodemus, it is absolutely radical and life changing. He's actually inviting us to enter into the realm of the kingdom of God that He's been preaching about. As we've already seen in the first section, the kingdom of God is in the realm of the Spirit, and this spiritual birth places us into that realm. As we're born again of the Spirit, we're actually taken out of the kingdom of darkness and brought into His wonderful light (see 1 Peter 2:9).

> *For he has rescued us from the dominion of darkness and brought us into the kingdom of the Son he loves* (Colossians 1:13 NIV).

> *[The Father] has delivered and drawn us to Himself out of the control and the dominion of darkness and has transferred us into the kingdom of the Son of His love* (Colossians 1:13 AMP).

When we hear the good news of the kingdom and make Jesus our King, the kingdom of God advances in the earth by advancing into us. This born-again experience isn't just saying a rote prayer, believing a doctrine, or joining a church. Rather, it's an encounter with God that is absolutely revolutionary.

This isn't to be confused with simply getting a second chance in your life either. This is a brand-new beginning where old things are passed away and all things become new. The new birth is more than just the place where we enter the kingdom and the kingdom comes to us. It is also the place of beginning an incredible adventure with the King Himself and learning how to walk in relationship with Him. By allowing Jesus to disciple us, we'll soon be praying kingdom prayers, seeking first the kingdom of God, and speaking the words and doing the works of Jesus. Our focus won't be consumed with waiting to go to Heaven, but we'll be learning to co-labor with the King to see His kingdom come here on the earth as it is in Heaven.

The greatest discovery of the new birth is the subject of our next chapter where we'll explore our new identity that flows

from our Heavenly Father.

Questions to Ponder

1. Have you personally felt the effects of "spiritual amnesia" in your life? Please explain.

2. How does being "born again" begin to deal with the issue of identity in your life?

3. Why do you feel the term "born again" deals with the issues of identity more than the term "salvation"?

CHAPTER 9

ABBA FATHER—HOME AT LAST

The second paradigm shift came upon me as suddenly as the first one. The Spirit had been hovering over me for some time, and there was a deep cry and longing going on within my spirit—a cry for *something* I had no language for. I knew *something* was coming my way. This has been true for most of the shifts that the Lord has brought into my life over the years. He first places a hunger and cry within my spirit, and then He comes along and fulfills that longing with a greater revelation of Himself.

Though I felt like much of my life and ministry was in a fairly healthy place during this season, the cry increased within me more and more, and tears would flow at the oddest of times. I knew in my spirit that the *something* was coming closer. Feeling it was time to get away, I decided to attend a conference with Jerry Cook, the author of *Love, Acceptance and Forgiveness*. Though Jerry's message during the first session was awesome as usual, what happened in the next meeting was what the Lord had been preparing my heart for. As the session opened, a young lady began to sing a chorus over us that absolutely exploded within me and hurled me into another *suddenly* with God.

> Abba Father, Abba Father
> Deep within my soul I cry
> Abba Father, Abba Father
> I will never cease to love You.

As she sang the chorus again and again, the very life of God seemed to enter into the words and wash over me with waves of love. As each wave hit me, the words "Abba Father" came with greater intensity and began to bring a freedom into my spirit I never dreamed was possible.

What happened to me for the next thirty minutes was an encounter with God that is still difficult to put into words. Though I'm sure any observer in the room would have only seen a sobbing mass of quivering jelly on the floor, it was much more than that. In those moments, God was answering the deepest cries of the human heart within me—cries to be loved and accepted by Father God. Though I had given my life to the Lord many years earlier, this was a completely different encounter. This wasn't about my sins or Heaven or eternal life. This was about *identity* and *destiny*. I am a son of God, and I had finally come home—home to the Father's heart.

Destination: Father

Part of the problem with the gospel of salvation is that it continually fuels the concept that Heaven is our destination. Now, don't get me wrong here. I love Heaven, and I'm looking forward to going there one day. But is Heaven where Jesus is really trying to take us? Every Christian knows that Jesus is the Way. But the way to where?

Thomas said to him, "Lord, we don't know where you are going, so how can we know the way?" Jesus answered, "I am the way and the truth and the life. No one comes to the Father except through me (John 14:5-6 NIV).

Did you catch that? Jesus didn't say, "I'm the way to Heaven"; He said, "I'm the way to the Father." Of course we still get Heaven because that's where the Father is, but Heaven was never meant to be the destination, and it can never satisfy the deepest cries of the human heart. *We weren't created for a place. We were created for a relationship with our Father, the living God.* Jesus goes so far as to tell us that eternal life is found in knowing the Father, not in going to Heaven. At the moment we are born again, God becomes our Father and we become His children. We were actually born into sonship. We didn't earn it, we don't deserve it, and we can't repay it.

> *Jesus didn't say, "I'm the way to heaven"; He said, "I'm the way to the Father."*
> ~

How great is the love the Father has lavished on us, that we should be called children of God! And that is what we are! (1 John 3:1a NIV).

But whoever did want him, who believed he was who he claimed and would do what he said, He made to be their true selves, their child-of-God selves. These are the God-begotten, not blood-begotten, not flesh-begotten, not sex-begotten (John 1:12-13 MSG).

I love how the Message version words it: *"He made to be their true selves, their child-of-God selves."* That's the identity that the

Father is trying to bring us into.

The Father Accepted and Affirmed Jesus

Jesus is the model and prototype for all believers. He's what the Scriptures call the *"firstborn among many brothers"* and it's His image and likeness we're being transformed into (Romans 8:29 NIV). In His incarnation, Jesus laid aside being God and became 100 percent man. In Him, we see what God intended for all mankind to be like in the original creation. As we saw in Chapter 3, identity was one of the lost things that Jesus came to restore. So let's briefly take a look at Jesus and His identity as a son of God.

> As Jesus was coming up out of the water, he saw heaven being torn open and the Spirit descending on him like a dove. And a voice came from heaven: "You are my Son, whom I love; with you I am well pleased" (Mark 1:10-11 NIV).

Here we see Jesus being baptized by John and the Spirit of God coming upon Him. After that, a voice comes from Heaven and tells Him three things:

1. You are my son.

2. I love you.

3. I'm pleased with you.

The first thing He heard is crucial for all of us to understand. The voice didn't say, "This is my son," as if God were trying to convince those listening of His sonship. The voice spoke directly to Jesus and said, "You are my son." Like all of us, Jesus needed to hear this directly from the Father to establish the issue of identity once and for all.

The Father not only told Jesus He was His son but added that He loved Him and was well pleased with Him. We need to remember that Jesus heard this before He did any ministry at all. Jesus had never preached, healed, delivered, or ministered in any way, and the Father told Him He was pleased with Him and loved Him. Here Jesus is totally accepted and loved by the Father apart from anything that He had done or accomplished. From that point on, Jesus ministered *from* acceptance and not *for* it, and the same should be true for all His children.

Not only was identity as a son of God the first revelation Jesus received from the Father, it was also the first line of attack by the enemy. In the gospels of Matthew and Luke, Jesus was immediately taken into the wilderness and tempted by the devil after He received the revelation of sonship from the Father. In the wilderness, the enemy came to Jesus in two different situations and asked Him if He was the son of God. For years I had heard the wilderness encounter preached as Jesus being tempted with the "lust of the world, the lust of the eyes, and the pride of life." But the enemy's test was aimed at His very core by questioning His identity as the Son of God.

Jesus Reveals the Father

Since identity as the son of God is at the very core of the life and ministry of Jesus, it seems only fitting that He would do all He could to pass that same revelation on to us. We often say that Jesus came into the world to seek and to save the lost and to destroy the works of the enemy, but we rarely hear about Him coming to reveal the Father.

> *All things have been committed to me by my Father. No one knows the Son except the*

> *Father, and no one knows the Father except*
> *the Son and those to whom the Son chooses to*
> *reveal him* (Matthew 11:27 NIV).

> *No man has ever seen God at any time; the*
> *only unique Son, or the only begotten God,*
> *Who is in the bosom [in the intimate presence]*
> *of the Father, He has declared Him [He has*
> *revealed Him and brought Him out where He*
> *can be seen; He has interpreted Him and He*
> *has made Him known]* (John 1:18 AMP).

The revelation came to me as I was reading one day and was puzzled over one of the phrases Jesus used in His great prayer in John 17.

> *And this is eternal life, that they may know*
> *You, the only true God, and Jesus Christ*
> *whom You have sent. I have glorified You*
> *on the earth. I have finished the work which*
> *You have given Me to do. And now, O Father,*
> *glorify Me together with Yourself, with the*
> *glory which I had with You before the world*
> *was. I have manifested Your name to the men*
> *whom You have given Me out of the world.*
> *They were Yours, You gave them to Me, and*
> *they have kept Your word* (John 17:3-7 NKJV).

I already understood that eternal life is intimate and relational. What troubled me in my reading that day was the phrase, *"I have finished the work which You have given Me to do."* Up to this time I had always assumed that the work was Jesus dying for the sins of the world on the cross at Calvary. But His death on the cross was still one day away. So what was the work that Jesus had already finished, the work that God had given Him to do? I read on to see if Jesus gave any clues to the puzzle before me. This time I felt the Spirit light up the phrase, *"I have manifested Your name."*

This was beginning to sound cryptic to me now, but since I love puzzles I pondered the verses over and over again. I have finished the work…I have manifested Your name. What name? I'd read the New Testament over and over and didn't remember Jesus revealing some cosmic name of God—a revelation so important that Jesus would lift His face to the heavens and tell the Lord He finished the work.

In the next few moments my mind seemed to race through the New Testament, and I finally understood the work that Jesus had finished. *He had revealed the Father **to** His disciples.* I began to realize that this wasn't a revelation that could simply be taught by Jesus; it actually needed to be pursued by the disciples, and Jesus had been waiting for them to ask this question since John 14.

> Philip said, "Lord, show us the Father and we will be satisfied." Jesus replied, "Have I been with you all this time, Philip, and yet you still don't know who I am? Anyone who has seen me has seen the Father! (John 14:8-9 NLT)

Here are the disciples with the best teacher, preacher, prophet, evangelist, miracle worker, and pastor with them on a daily basis, and yet their cry is, *"Show us the Father and we will be satisfied."* Could it be that this cry to see and know the Father is actually a universal cry of all humanity? I believe Jesus was waiting for this request to be made, for the rest of His plan couldn't go into effect until it had. Jesus needed

> *Jesus said, "If you have seen me, you've seen the father."*
> ～

to pass something on to His disciples, which would endure through the ages and be passed on to future generations. He wasn't establishing a Bible school, handing out doctrines and creeds, or talking about church growth principles and methodologies. He knew if He could pass on to His disciples an identity that flows from a relationship with the Father, the rest would fall into place.

Jesus responds to Philip with one of the crowning revelations of the New Testament, *If you have seen me, you've seen the Father.* Jesus is the spitting image of His Father—the Father with skin on. He is the walking will of God among us.

> *We look at this Son and see the God who cannot be seen. We look at this Son and see God's original purpose in everything created* (Colossians 1:15 MSG).

> *The Son is the radiance of God's glory and the exact representation of his being* (Hebrews 1:3 NIV).

When Jesus concludes His prayer in the Garden of Gethsemane, He confirms that all of our identity is wrapped up in the love of the Father.

> *And I have declared to them Your name, and will declare it, that the love with which You loved Me may be in them, and I in them* (John 17:26 NKJV).

Next, we will take a look at how God's love solidifies our identity in the Father.

Questions to Ponder

1. How have you processed the change from destination Heaven to destination Father?

2. How have you found your way (or been lead) to know the Father's heart for you?

3. Are the works you are doing in God for His acceptance or from it? Give an example.

Chapter 10

How Great is His Love

In times of shift and change, our congregation discovered the incredible faithfulness of the Lord to lead us onward in the journey of uncovering what He wanted us to find. Some of the ways He led us were familiar like the revelations in His Word and the still, small voice, but as prayer and a hunger for His presence increased, He began to speak to us in ways that were common in the Bible, yet new to us. As the book of Job puts it, *"For God does speak—now one way, now another—though man may not perceive it"* (Job 33:14 NIV). As His presence increased in our midst, people began to have dreams and visions, angels were appearing, prophetic words were being received, nature was speaking louder, and some even began to hear His audible voice through mysterious encounters. Though the Lord spoke many times to us during this season, two incidents encouraged us greatly in seeking and understanding our new identity in Christ.

The first incident was very encouraging and powerful and came to me in a brief dream one night. I dreamt about a men's workday at the church. Many of the men from our fellowship were doing various jobs in our church building. Suddenly, I was drawn to a man that I had never seen before. I went over to him and asked him whom he was and what he was doing there. He simply responded, *"I'm the electrician. I've come to rewire the building."* Then I woke up.

Shortly after the dream, the Lord spoke again to my heart during one of our weekly prayer meetings. We had been praying for a while and crying out for more of His Spirit as we had done many times before when suddenly a question came into my mind, *"What would it look like if the Spirit did come?"* All of a sudden I realized I was praying for something that I wouldn't even know or recognize should it come into the room and bite me. Sensing the Lord was asking me the question to lead me into something (and not just to make me look stupid), I quieted my heart before Him. A few minutes later the following verses from the gospel of John flooded my mind:

> *And when He has come, He will convict the world of sin, and of righteousness, and of judgment: of sin, because they do not believe in Me; of righteousness, because I go to My Father and you see Me no more; of judgment, because the ruler of this world is judged* (John 16:8-11 NKJV).

After pondering the dream and the verses from John, I felt the Lord was preparing me for even more of a paradigm shift in the area of identity. Having been wrongly wired by religious traditions and humanistic thinking, I had no sense of my true identity, which led to a life void of the power of God. As I considered the words from John, the Spirit was strongly highlighting portions of verses I had never seen before. Up to this point I only knew that the Spirit had come to convict me of sin for not believing in Jesus.

Now I saw that He wanted to convince me of my righteousness in Jesus with that same intensity, and that the enemy had been completely judged through the work of Jesus at the cross. In other words, the Spirit of God interacting in my life would convince me of my identity rooted in the righteousness of Christ. Flowing out of this conviction would be the ability to exercise the power and authority given to me over the enemy because he was judged and defeated. The exciting thing about the light shed on these verses was that I could now recognize that all three of these things were already happening in the midst of our fellowship at that time, and that meant that the Spirit of God was already here!

He Loves Us Because He Is Love

In this paradigm shift of identity, I found myself having to deal a deathblow to some of the religious baggage I had picked up along the way. Though by this time I had been born again for over twelve years, I still had lingering thoughts of unworthiness and of not quite measuring up to the expectations that came from God-only-knows where. I've discovered that these same thoughts and feelings are at the very core of most religions and usually keep their followers, who have a shame-based identity, on a treadmill of religious performance. But Christianity isn't built on a shame-based identity; it is built on a righteousness-based identity. Our good and loving Father sent His only Son into the world to take upon himself our sin and shame, and in return, gave us the gift of righteousness—the very righteousness of God. Years after I finally shifted to a righteousness-based identity, the Lord gave me the following phrase to help me

> *The Spirit of God would convince me of my identity, which was rooted in the righteousness of Christ*
> ~

discern if I ever fall back into the grip of religion.

Religion says, "God will love you more if_____," and, "God loves you less because_____."

The blanks can be filled in with any religious idea, depending on the camp you have been living in. An example might be: God will love you more if you spend more time in prayer every day, or He loves you less because you watch TV.

God doesn't love any of us because we are loveable. He loves us because He is Love. The burden isn't on us to perform for the Father's love. He loves us based on who He is and not on who we are or what we have done. God isn't loving, as if He can turn it on and off; He is Love. It's His very nature. It's something we can all depend on as we tear down the strongholds in our minds and are renewed by the Spirit. His love is like the sun that shines. The sun doesn't shine on things because they are worthy of being shined on. It shines on them because it is the very nature of the sun. Any sin within doesn't stop God from loving us; it just releases His loving discipline. The following verses might shed some light on this and help in the process of mind renewal.

> *Jesus doesn't love any of us because we're loveable. He loves us because He is love.*
> ∾

> *How great is the love the Father has lavished on us, that we should be called children of God! And that is what we are!* (1 John 3:1a NIV).

> *And so we know and rely on the love God has for us. God is love. Whoever lives in love lives in God, and God in him* (1 John 4:16 NIV).

There is no fear in love. But perfect love drives out fear, because fear has to do with punishment. The one who fears is not made perfect in love. We love because he first loved us (1 John 4:18-19 NIV).

Who shall separate us from the love of Christ? Shall trouble or hardship or persecution or famine or nakedness or danger or sword? ...For I am convinced that neither death nor life, neither angels nor demons, neither the present nor the future, nor any powers, neither height nor depth, nor anything else in all creation, will be able to separate us from the love of God that is in Christ Jesus our Lord (Romans 8:35, 38-39 NIV).

No Longer a Sinner Saved by Grace

Who we are will determine what we will do. If this is true, the proverbial question, "Do we sin because we're sinners?" or "Are we sinners because we sin?" can only be answered in one way—we sin because we are sinners. If that last statement is true, the work of Jesus has to not only forgive us of our sins, but it has to change our nature at its very core also. Though most of our doctrines and theologies agree with this, there seems to be some splinters of unbelief on this second step that need to be sanded down so the Green Ladder can be properly restored.

On the evening of September 6, 1970, I gave my heart to the Lord. As a hippie (bearing the alias of the Stoned Wizard) I made my way to an old-fashioned altar and gave my heart and life to Jesus. It was there, on that most wonderful of all days, I joined the ranks of millions who had gone before me and became yet another sinner saved by grace.

If by the phrase "sinner saved by grace" we mean that incredible moment where God becomes our Father and we become His children, where we become a brand-new creation in Christ as we receive the righteousness of God and are translated out of the kingdom of darkness into His marvelous light, then the phrase will stand as one of the most beautiful flowers in our garden. However, if we view ourselves as *sinners* saved by grace, and we are forgiven for what we have done but not changed in who we are, then the term "sinner saved by grace" becomes a strangling weed in our garden.

In the New Testament, believers are not addressed as sinners; they are addressed as saints. If we are indeed saints, then God has not only forgiven us, but He's changed us at the very core of our being and our identity is altered. If we believe we are sinners saved by grace, much of the energy of the Church will be focused on sin management because we actually expect people to sin. If, on the other hand, we believe them to be saints, we'll expect them to act like saints, like sons and daughters of God. Let's read a few verses to see what the Word of God has to say on this subject.

> *Paul, an apostle of Jesus Christ by the will of God, to the saints who are in Ephesus, and faithful in Christ Jesus* (Ephesians 1:1 NKJV).

> *And I pray that you, being rooted and established in love, may have power, together with all the saints, to grasp how wide and long and high and deep is the love of Christ, and to know this love that surpasses knowledge— that you may be filled to the measure of all the fullness of God* (Ephesians 3:17-19 NIV).

Dear friends, although I was very eager to write to you about the salvation we share, I felt I had to write and urge you to contend for the faith that was once for all entrusted to the saints (Jude 3 NIV).

It may surprise you to know that the above verses aren't some rare, isolated cases of where believers are called "saints" in the New Testament. The term is actually used over sixty times to describe believers. When I discovered this, I was personally shocked because my paradigm was sinner oriented and not saint oriented, and I needed a radical shift to view the Church as God views it.

The Glorious Gift of Righteousness

The Gospel of the kingdom not only transitions us from being sinners to saints, it also shifts us from having a shame-based identity to having a righteousness-based identity. Just like the mud I saw on the Green Ladder, the religious buildup of guilt, shame, and condemnation has significantly paralyzed the church in the Western world. It must be removed if we are to step onto the third step of the Ladder where we become co-laborers with God for the release of His kingdom on the earth.

Though all religions agree we're supposed to be righteous, how someone actually becomes righteous is among the most heated of all religious questions—a question that only authentic Christianity can answer. While other religions offer a righteousness that is to be earned by keeping rules and standards, Christianity comes along with more good news, seemingly too good to be true. It offers us the *gift of righteousness.*

For if, by the trespass of the one man, death reigned through that one man, how

much more will those who receive God's
abundant provision of grace and of the gift
of righteousness reign in life through the one
man, Jesus Christ (Romans 5:17 NIV).

Since it is a gift of righteousness, it cannot be earned or purchased in any way because it comes to us by grace. Unlike mercy, where God doesn't give us what we deserve, grace is that incredible New Testament word that means God gives us what we don't deserve. So the righteousness we receive isn't earned or deserved by keeping the Law or being good. It is a gift offered to us by the Lord and is received by believing the promise by faith. And faith pleases God more than all our self-righteous works.

But now a righteousness from God, apart from
law, has been made known, to which the Law
and the Prophets testify. This righteousness
from God comes through faith in Jesus Christ
to all who believe (Romans 3:21-22 NIV).

What really amazes me about the righteousness that God gives us is that He does much more than simply declare us righteous. He actually gives us His righteousness. That's right! Jesus not only took our sins at the cross, but He actually became the very essence of sin so that in and through Him we could have the righteousness of God.

For our sake He made Christ [virtually] to be
sin Who knew no sin, so that in and through
Him we might become [endued with, viewed as
being in, and examples of] the righteousness
of God [what we ought to be, approved and
acceptable and in right relationship with
Him, by His goodness] (2 Corinthians 5:21
AMP).

In my pre-Christian days I used to get upset when people told me that the entire human race fell with Adam when he sinned in the Garden. They told me that we all became sinners because of the actions of Adam. In other words, Adam made me a sinner. As much as I hated that reasoning when I was far from God, I have come to appreciate it since I have become a Christian. I have discovered that in the same way I was made a sinner by the actions of Adam, I have now been made righteous by the actions of Jesus.

> For just as through the disobedience of the one man the many were made sinners, so also through the obedience of the one man the many will be made righteous (Romans 5:19 NIV).

So the gospel of the kingdom not only brings us out of the kingdom of darkness and into His light, it also has the power to change us on the inside and shift us from having a sinner/shame-based identity to having a saint/righteousness-based identity. This new identity has nothing to do with who we are or what we've done; it's based solely on *whose* we are. We are the sons and daughters of God.

Though the English word for *saint* is usually linked to an individual's character and pious deeds, the word in the Greek connotes ownership by God, those who have been set apart by God and for God, or the consecrated ones. Being called saints and possessing the righteousness of God is based solely on our belief in what Jesus has done for us at the cross. We didn't earn it, we don't deserve it, and we can't repay it, but we can surely live our lives as saints.

All these revelations are part of the dream in which the electrician rewired our building. To have a Christianity where we believe our sins are forgiven, but are not convinced that our nature is changed, leads to an ineffective and frustrating Christian life. If we only believed that our sins are forgiven, we might still be operating from a sinner/shame-based identity and walking on the treadmill of religious performance. But the electrician in the dream is the Holy Spirit that brings about transformation in our lives by bringing renewal to our minds by the Spirit and the Word. From the very moment we were born again, we became saints and children of God in complete possession of His righteousness. Even though these statements are true and should lead to our freedom, we may not come into the necessary paradigm shift for years if we are constantly abiding in a sinner/shame-based environment; one that constantly tells us, "God will love you more if_____," and, "God loves you less because_____."

In the next chapter we'll discover the power of being IN Christ.

Questions to Ponder

1. Why does God love you?

2. How have you come to believe you are a saint, and how does that effect your relationship to God and others?

3. What religious baggage are you learning to throw out so that you get off the treadmill of performance and into knowing you have the righteousness of God?

CHAPTER 11

THE INCREDIBLENESS
OF BEING IN CHRIST

Of all the different learning environments available to us today, I would have to say my personal favorite is question and answer time. Whether it is one-on-one mentoring or a session at a large conference where speakers field questions from the crowd, the precious pearls shared in these times are the most rewarding to me. During the early days of the Vineyard Movement, the Lord began to highlight to me the incredible power of the word "in" when John Wimber responded to one of the questions asked of him during a pastor's conference. Though most of the questions fielded by John that day were focused on the present move of the Spirit and the kingdom of God, someone in the crowd asked for his views on the doctrine of eternal security. Though most of the people present that day could not have cared less about this question, a curious silence came into the room as the audience waited to see how John would respond to this theological booby trap.

After a few moments, John finally put the microphone to

his mouth and simply said, *"Stay in the plane."* After allowing hte idea to penetrate for a few moments, John illuminated his answer by encouraging us to simply remain *in Christ* and explore all that is truly ours *in Him*, instead of spending our time trying to figure out if there's a way to get out of the place where God has placed us which is *in Christ.*

After John's simple response, I began to investigate the many Scriptures with the phrase *in Christ* or *in Him* and was amazed at the power of this incredible revelation that had been given to the apostle Paul. During this season of discovery, the Lord illustrated this truth to me at an even deeper level by reminding me of an experience I had when I was eighteen. At that time, I was scheduled for oral surgery to have a tooth removed that had become infected at the root.

As I sat in the chair in the surgeon's office with the intravenous anesthetic hooked up to my arm, the nurse asked me to count slowly backwards from one hundred. Having been raised with the spy pictures of the '60s, I had seen this done many times and was really excited. I felt I could probably count all the way down to at least fifty. In spite of my strong will and determination, I only made it to ninety-eight. The next thing I remember was waking up in the office chair and asking the nurse, *"When are you going to do the operation?"* Her response shocked me when she said, *"We already did."*

Many years after that event, the Lord quickened the following verse to me that I have treasured for a long time.

> *Buried with him in baptism, wherein also ye are risen with him through the faith of the operation of God, who hath raised him from the dead* (Colossians 2:12 KJV).

Did you catch the phrase, *"faith of the operation of God?"*

Other translations say, *"faith in the workings of God,"* or *"faith in the power of God."* Thousands of years ago God performed an incredible operation that actually placed us *in Christ*. It doesn't really matter if we remember the operation or not. It has been done and we actually are *in* Christ. God, once again, did His part and now all we need to do is have faith in the operation God performed. After all, that's how we all came to be born again in the first place, and the *way in* is to be the *way on.*

We are in Christ—We are not on Probation

Being placed in Christ is one of the central themes developed in the New Testament. It is the deep and solid root of the saint/righteousness-based identity we received when we were born again and became brand-new creations as the sons and daughters of God. First Corinthians 12 actually says the Spirit has baptized us into the body of Christ.

> *For as the body is one and has many members, but all the members of that one body, being many, are one body, so also is Christ. For by one Spirit we were all baptized into one body—whether Jews or Greeks, whether slaves or free—and have all been made to drink into one Spirit* (1 Corinthians 12:12-13 NKJV).

It is a violation of Scripture and God's intent to think that the Holy Spirit is picking up dirty pieces of humanity and placing them into the holy body of Christ. At the new birth, we are not only forgiven and washed from our sins (what we have done), but we have also been changed at the very core of our being (who we are).

If we embrace a Christianity that gives us a sinner/shame-based identity, we are more often put on probation instead of being placed into Christ. Probation says we have been let out of jail, but we go back to prison if we mess up again. If we believe we are forgiven for what we've done, but still a sinner at our core, we will spend most of our life focusing on our performance and justifying our failures with such phrases as, "We're only human."

But we are not on probation. We are in Christ. As to "being only human," nothing could be further from the truth. It's time we realize we are more than just people who have been given a second chance. Authentic Christianity is about Jesus regaining for mankind what Adam lost for us in the Garden. Adam didn't earn the right to be in the image of God; he was created that way, and the same is true for every person who is born again. God didn't abort His first plan. He still intends to make us into His likeness and image so that we can co-labor with Him to expand the kingdom. Because we have been so thoroughly immersed in a religious, sinner/shame-based culture, any teaching that hints at us being like Christ at all is usually met with fear and warnings of New Age deception.

> *Adam didn't earn the right to be in the image of God; he was created that way.*

Let's look at a few verses in the New Testament that lift the bar a lot higher for us in this area, verses that lean more towards our destiny in God than our ability to earn or obtain righteousness through performance.

> *For those God foreknew he also predestined to be conformed to the likeness of his Son, that he might be the firstborn among many brothers* (Romans 8:29 NIV).

> *And just as we have borne the likeness of the earthly man, so shall we bear the likeness of*

the man from heaven (1 Corinthians 15:49 NIV).

That you may be filled to the measure of all the fullness of God (Ephesians 3:19 NIV).

Until we all reach unity in the faith and in the knowledge of the Son of God and become mature, attaining to the whole measure of the fullness of Christ (Ephesians 4:13 NIV).

And you have been given fullness in Christ, who is the head over every power and authority (Colossians 2:9-10 NIV).

And to put on the new self, created to be like God in true righteousness and holiness (Ephesians 4:24 NIV).

Dear friends, now we are children of God, and what we will be has not yet been made known. But we know that when he appears, we shall be like him, for we shall see him as he is (1 John 3:2 NIV).

The Last Adam—The Second Man

As the Lord began to shed light on the subject of being *in Christ*, I began to wonder at what point believers were actually placed in Him. For instance, were we placed in Him in the very beginning when He was the living Word and spoke the worlds into existence, or were we placed in Him at His incarnation? Or maybe we were placed in Him when John baptized him and the Spirit came upon Him, or later in the wilderness temptations or during His prayer in the Garden. I felt the Lord was encouraging me to go after the pieces of this puzzle, so I will spend the rest of this chapter unpacking this revelation in its abridged version.

I found the first piece of the puzzle in Romans 6.

> *Or don't you know that all of us who were*
> *baptized into Christ Jesus were baptized into*
> *his death?* (Romans 6:3 NIV).

From this verse I saw that when anyone placed their faith in Jesus they were then placed into Him at the moment of His death on the cross. Though this seemed to answer my question as to what point in Christ's life we were placed in Him, I didn't understand the significance of it and asked the Lord for more pieces of the puzzle. He then led me to a rich portion of Scripture found in First Corinthians that really helped me to unravel this mystery further.

> *So it is written: "The first man Adam became*
> *a living being"; the last Adam, a life-giving*
> *spirit. The spiritual did not come first, but the*
> *natural, and after that the spiritual. The first*
> *man was of the dust of the earth, the second*
> *man from heaven. As was the earthly man,*
> *so are those who are of the earth; and as is*
> *the man from heaven, so also are those who*
> *are of heaven. And just as we have borne*
> *the likeness of the earthly man, so shall we*
> *bear the likeness of the man from heaven* (1
> Corinthians 15:45-49 NIV).

The labels given to Adam and Jesus were what puzzled me most in these texts. Adam was called the first Adam and the first man. This seemed obvious to me and made perfect sense. But why was Jesus called the Last Adam and the Second Man and not the Second Adam and the Second Man? The language seemed to make Jesus a doorway—out of one place and into another.

Adam	Jesus
Known as the First Man and the First Adam.	Known as the Second Man and the Last Adam.
Begins the Adamic race.	Ends the Adamic race by dying as a perfect man. This is the cross/crucifixion side of Christianity.
Also called the First Man – of the earth.	As the Second Man, Jesus welcomes us into the spirit and resurrection side of Christianity.
Through Adam we are all born into sin.	Through Jesus we are reborn; He is the doorway out of the first Adam's nature and into the nature of the Second Man.
As Adam's children, we inherit a sin nature.	Through faith in Jesus, our sinful nature is put to death and we receive a heavenly inheritance, communion with the Holy Spirit, and resurrection power.

Being the Last Adam seemed to suggest He was going to end the Adamic race. On the other side of that door He would be the Second Man. From God's perspective there are really only two men, and all of us are either in Adam or in Jesus. But in order to get in Jesus the Second Man, we first need to be found in Jesus the Last Adam. The Last Adam is the cross/crucifixion side of Christianity, which is why we are baptized into His death. The Second Man is the Spirit/resurrection side. In other words, all that we were in the first Adam is put to death in Jesus, the Last Adam, at the cross. Consequently, all that Jesus is, in the Second Man, becomes ours by the Holy Spirit. The first puts *us in Christ* through the shedding of His blood; the second puts *Christ in us* because of His resurrection. The first *cleanses the vessel*, and the second *fills the vessel.*

Theologians use a phrase, "Federal Head," that might help us a little here. This phrase basically means that any decision I make has consequences on all my future offspring. For instance, if I leave Oregon and move to New York, all my future offspring have moved to New York with me because their seed is still in me. Chapter five of Romans tells us that when Adam sinned and let death enter the world, all mankind sinned and died also because they were in Adam. In Hebrews 7, Scripture records that Levi paid a tithe to Melchizedek through Abraham, because Levi, still unborn, was in the body of Abraham. This truth comes home for us in First Corinthians 15:22 where it says, *"For as in Adam all die, even so in Christ shall all be made alive"* (KJV).

The last piece of this puzzle is a little nugget that's tucked away in the book of Acts. This verse will shed some light on Jesus as the Second Man.

> We tell you the good news: What God promised our fathers he has fulfilled for us, their children, by raising up Jesus. As it is written in the second Psalm: "You are my Son; today I have become your Father" (Acts 13:32-33 NIV).

This is one of those *read it again for the first time* verses. Though we have already heard *"You are my Son"* at His baptism and at the Mount of Transfiguration, it is different this time. Here the Spirit reaches into the second Psalm and declares not only the resurrection of Jesus from the dead, but also boldly proclaims, *"You are my Son; today I have become your Father."* Without trying to start some kind of doctrinal riot, it almost seems as if Jesus was somehow born again the day He rose from the dead. In fact, on several occasions the New Testament declares that Jesus is the *firstborn from among the dead.* I'm wondering if this is a clue to the language used in the verses we just looked at in First Corinthians 15. Though I don't see myself as a biblical scholar, it sure looks like He died on the cross as the Last Adam and then rose from the dead as the Second Man.

The good news in all this is that the Scriptures tell us we were baptized (or placed into Christ) at the cross, and we were crucified, buried, and rose with Him. However we view it, we are no longer in Adam, nor are we on probation. We are in Christ and He is in us. Our entire identity is in Him, and to look for it elsewhere is a contradiction of New Testament revelation.

Another rendering of First Corinthians 15:49 is seen in many of the footnotes of various translations:

> And just as we have borne the likeness of the
> earthly man, **let us also bear** the likeness of the
> man from heaven (NIV).

Next, we'll look at several different names given to the church that will add depth to our identity and clarify what we ought to be doing.

Questions to Ponder

1. What does the phrase "the way in is to be the way on" mean to you?

2. What is the significance of the word "in" when it comes to your identity?

3. Explain how being in Jesus the last Adam and the second Man has altered your view of your identity.

CHAPTER 12

NAMES THAT REVEAL OUR IDENTITY

Earlier in this section I mentioned that much of the identity crisis facing the church today is correlated with our spiritual amnesia. We have forgotten who we are, where we have come from, and what we are supposed to be doing. It's interesting that one of the first questions that those with amnesia ask is, *"Who am I?"* They're hoping someone can tell them their name and give them some sense of who they are. Unfortunately for us, names in our culture are often labels and give us very little insight into our identity.

For instance, my name, Steve Shaw, doesn't give any hint as to who I really am, what I do, or what my character traits are. But a name in the Bible often speaks volumes about one's identity, destiny, and character. There we find Abraham is the *father of many nations* (see Genesis 17:5), Isaac is *laughter* (see Genesis 21:3, 6), Jacob is a *supplanter* (see Genesis 25:26), and David is *my beloved*.[1] Even our Lord is given two names at His birth, Jesus and Immanuel, signifying that He's the *Savior*[2] and *God with us*.[3]

So what about the names given to the Church in the New Testament? Each name is a declaration by God that reveals one of the many facets of our new identity in Christ. Each of these names, like facets on a gem, adds to the picture of who we are, and what we are supposed to be doing.

Our fellowship began studying the names given to the Church in Scripture, and we felt our corporate identity shift as we started praying and proclaiming these names over ourselves. It wasn't long after we came into agreement with who God said we are, that faith arose and we actually started acting like who He said we are.

As we looked at the different names of the Church found in the New Testament, we discovered that their original meaning was to be an extension of God Himself. We are His body, His army, His priests, etc. Sure, humanity receives great benefits as the Church begins to function the way He designed it to, but the Church doesn't exist just to serve itself or even humanity; it exists for God. That was another paradigm shift for our fellowship. We actually had a Sunday morning where we began to proclaim, *"This one [this church] is for God! This one is for God!"*

> We are His body, His army, His priests.
> ∾

We Are *His* Church

This may sound like a strange starting place to some, but it really is **His** church, and coming to understand the origin and meaning of this word in the Scriptures will bring clarity to the other names given to the church.

> *"But what about you?" he asked. "Who do you say I am?" Simon Peter answered, "You are the Christ, the Son of the living God." Jesus*

replied, "Blessed are you, Simon son of Jonah,
for this was not revealed to you by man, but
by my Father in heaven. And I tell you that
you are Peter, and on this rock I will build
my church, and the gates of Hades will not
overcome it. I will give you the keys of the
kingdom of heaven; whatever you bind on
earth will be bound in heaven, and whatever
you loose on earth will be loosed in heaven"
(Matthew 16:15-19 NIV).

This is the first use of the word church in the New Testament and is really the key to understanding all other names given to the church. The basic meaning of the word *church* is *the called out ones.*[4] As seen in the Matthew text, the church is built upon the rock, the revelation that Jesus is the Son of God, the Christ, the promised Messiah, the Lord of Lords, and the King of Kings.

As each of us embraces the rock revelation, we are born again and become a member of the church, part of the community of the called out ones. Jesus gives His church the keys of the kingdom of Heaven. He then commissions us to advance His rule and reign on the earth and assures us that even the gates of hell won't be able to stop His empowered church.

We Are His Holy and Royal Priests

You also, like living stones, are being built
into a spiritual house to be a holy priesthood,
offering spiritual sacrifices acceptable to God
through Jesus Christ (1 Peter 2:5 NIV).

But you are a chosen people, a royal
priesthood, a holy nation, a people belonging
to God, that you may declare the praises of

him who called you out of darkness into his
wonderful light (1 Peter 2:9 NIV).

This name for the church, a royal priesthood, is finally being recovered to the body of Christ after years of overreacting to the misuse of the word in the Catholic Church. Be assured, we are His priests. As priests, our first ministry is unto the Lord with spiritual sacrifices of praise, worship, intercession, and petitions to the God of heaven to release His kingdom on the earth.

Understand that when God asks us to give Him a sacrifice of praise, He is not asking us for something we don't have but for something we have and may not want to give. The sacrificial praises of the priests actually set up a habitation for God on the earth because *"He inhabits the praises of His people"* (see Psalm 22:3 KJV).

We Are His Temple

In him the whole building is joined together
and rises to become a holy temple in the Lord.
And in him you too are being built together to
become a dwelling in which God lives by his
Spirit (Ephesians 2:21-22 NIV).

You realize, don't you, that you are the temple
of God, and God himself is present in you? (1
Corinthians 3:16-17 MSG).

It may seem odd, but we are not just the priests of God. We are also His temple. Every building has a purpose, and the purpose of the Church is to be a habitation for God in the earth. Temples are places of worship, and that is exactly what the Lord is looking for in His temple. But His temple isn't limited to some fixed street address; we are a moveable dwelling place for God to inhabit 24/7 wherever we are. We will do well to remember that a single brick, or even a pile of bricks doesn't make a building. To be His dwelling place, we will need to be cemented together in covenant love with other living stones.

We Are His Family

> Now you are no longer strangers to God and foreigners to heaven, but you are members of God's very own family, citizens of God's country, and you belong in God's household with every other Christian (Ephesians 2:19 TLB).

We have yet to see the power that God has in store for the Church when we discover and act out what it means to be His family. In the '90s, the Spirit was bringing forth a fresh revelation of the Father's heart for His children, and that same

> *It's time for us to embrace the Spirit that was upon Joseph who recognized his brothers even though they didn't recognize Him.*
> ∽

Spirit is crying out today to see the Father's love demonstrated as we restore the command of Christ *to love one another as He loved us.* It's time for us to embrace the Spirit that was upon Joseph *who recognized his brothers even though they didn't recognize Him* (see Genesis 42:7).

It is a blessing to see the church today rallying around apostolic fathers, those who honor individuals for their unique contribution to the body of Christ and seek to empower all to walk in their God-given destiny. Believers from many theological backgrounds are coming together in conferences and meetings.

It is not because their doctrinal statements align perfectly, but because something resonates in them. They recognize that these fathers have their heartbeat, speak their language, and that this is their family.

We see seemingly every denomination present enjoying the Father and His family where blessings are poured out on family relationship and unity instead of doctrinal distinctives. John puts it bluntly in his first letter when he tells them, *"Don't tell me you love God, who you can't see, when you don't love your brother who you can see"* (1 John 4:20, author's paraphrase) We actually love the Father when we love His Family.

We Are His Body

> *And God placed all things under his feet and appointed him to be head over everything for the church, which is his body, the fullness of him who fills everything in every way* (Ephesians 1:22-23 NIV).

> *He is in charge of it all, has the final word on everything. At the center of all this, Christ rules the church. The church, you see, is not peripheral to the world; the world is peripheral to the church. The church is Christ's body, in which he speaks and acts, by which he fills everything with his presence* (Ephesians 1:22-23 MSG).

This is probably the most profound of all the names given to the Church, and is the only one that is not represented in the Old Testament with a shadow of what was to come.[5] Each believer is a member of the body of Christ and has an important function to perform. Through the Great Commission and the outpouring of the Holy Spirit, Jesus passed the baton to the church to continue doing what He did.

We are to speak His words, do His work, and walk His walk. As Bill Johnson put so beautifully, *"We are to represent, or re-present Christ in the earth."* We are actually Jesus with skin on and are to be the answer to the Greeks that came to Philip and said, *"We would like to see Jesus"* (John 12:20-21).

We Are His Army

> *And I will put enmity between you and the woman, and between your offspring and hers; he will crush your head, and you will strike his heel* (Genesis 3:15 NIV).

> *Endure hardship with us like a good soldier of Christ Jesus* (2 Timothy 2:3 NIV).

The very first prophecy in the Bible hurls the Church into a cosmic war between the kingdom of darkness and His glorious Light (see Genesis 3:15). We were born again as soldiers in His Army. We were born for battle. It's who we are. It's what we do. We are to be the Church that the gates of hell won't be able to stand against. Jeremiah gives the following warning to us concerning what he calls the Lord's work:

> *A curse on him who is lax in doing the LORD's work! A curse on him who keeps his sword from bloodshed!* (Jeremiah 48:10 NIV).

We Are His Sheep

> *I am the good shepherd; I know my sheep and my sheep know me...My sheep listen to my*

voice; I know them, and they follow me (John
10:14, 27 NIV).

This one is fairly simple. We are His sheep that are to know
Him and be known by Him. As His sheep, it is not enough to
simply study Him. We are to be listening for His voice and
following Him wherever He would lead us. Jesus isn't just tending
His flock. He is leading it!

We Are His Ambassadors

> *We are therefore Christ's ambassadors, as
> though God were making his appeal through
> us. We implore you on Christ's behalf: Be
> reconciled to God* (2 Corinthians 5:20 NIV).

As His Ambassadors, we are the liaisons between the kingdom
of God and those still captured in the kingdom of darkness.
As we carry His presence into this world, we are like moveable
embassies that speak and act on the King's behalf, offering people
sanctuary in the kingdom of God.

We Are His Bride

> *One of the seven angels who had the seven
> bowls full of the seven last plagues came and
> said to me, "Come, I will show you the bride,
> the wife of the Lamb"* (Revelation 21:9 NIV).

> *The marriage relationship is doubtless a
> great mystery, but I am speaking of something
> deeper still—the marriage of Christ and His
> church* (Ephesians 5:32 Phillips).

As His bride, the Spirit is revealing an even deeper level of relationship to the church, and words like passion, intimacy, and bridal love are being added to our vocabulary. Much like Eve was to Adam in the Garden, we have been created for Jesus to be both His bride and helper. We are the ones who are to be the closest to His heart, the recipients of His love, and the bearers of His glory. Because the bride is being fueled by love instead of duty, fear, or obligation, she is able to come into a deeper level of radical obedience than either a servant or friend could.

We Are His Branches

I am the vine; you are the branches. If a man remains in me and I in him, he will bear much fruit; apart from me you can do nothing (John 15:5 NIV).

When we think of being branches in the Vine, one word says it all: **dependence!** Abiding in Him and drawing from Him is something that happens moment by moment. Only as we return to complete and total dependence on Christ will we bear genuine fruit in our lives. The beauty of this picture is that it is hard to know where the Vine ends and the branches begin.

So there you have it. The church is a multifaceted gem, and each of the facets brings out different aspects of our identity and declares who we are and what we should be doing. We are an army to fight, a body to function, priests to minister, and so on.

> *Abiding in Him and drawing from Him is something that happens moment by moment.*
> ~

Before I leave this section, I would like to insert a small caution. Allow the Spirit to bring you into the fullness of your identity in Christ as described in the various names He has for the Church. Don't settle for just your favorite names or what you feel matches your personality.

These are facets on a gem, and no one facet makes up the entire gem. We are His bride, but we are more than His bride. We are His body, yet we are more than His body. As no single name for God reveals all that He is and does, so it is with the Church. The full revelation of the Church is more encompassing than the sum of all its parts.

Let's move on to the final step of the Green Ladder, where we take the message of the kingdom of God and our identity in Christ and learn to co-labor with a sovereign God.

Questions to Ponder

1. What names of the church do you identify with most readily? Why?

2. What names given to the church mean the most to you and why?

3. How do you stay dependent on God as Leader in your life?

STEP 3

CO-LABORING WITH GOD

CHAPTER 13

REMOVING WEEDS FROM SOVEREIGNTY'S GARDEN

In this final section, we are going to uncover the last step of the Green Ladder, where we begin to co-labor with our Sovereign God to advance His kingdom on earth. Whereas the first step of the Ladder gave us the message of the kingdom of God, and the second step the identity of the people of the kingdom, this last step empowers Saints to action. But before we can restore this final step of the Ladder, we first have to remove some of the weeds that have grown up in our theological gardens. These weeds have given us a distorted view of the sovereignty of God.

The year was 1970, and I was a brand-new Christian with all the life and joy of someone who had just come into the presence of God. My prayers at that time had the innocence of a child—fresh, honest, and unreligious. It seemed that they were answered as fast as I could pray them, and my attitude was simply that nothing is too difficult for my God.

It was about this time in my Christian walk that I began to

hear about what I have now come to call a distorted view of the sovereignty of God. Simply put, this teaching said that God is the cause of everything that has ever happened. He knows all, controls all, is over all, and has caused all. This threw me into a spiritual whirlwind that began to destroy the newfound life and faith I was enjoying in Jesus.

My mind began to wonder why I should pray for someone to be saved since the sovereign God had already determined who would be saved. Did my prayers have any affect upon a sovereign God at all, or were they simply an exercise in religious futility? And what about free will? Could we chose to be saved or was that all predetermined by the sovereignty of God also?

As my mind was spinning with thoughts about God's sovereignty during this season, the church I was attending invited some missionaries to come and share one night. They seemed like incredibly wise and simple servants of the King, so I figured I would share with them the difficulties I was having with the sovereignty of God.

I posed a scenario of going into Baskin Robbins to get some ice cream. Though I went in with the intent to get some Nutty Coconut, at the last second I changed my mind and picked Jamoca Almond Fudge. I then asked them if I ended up with the Jamoca Almond Fudge because of the sovereignty of God or simply because I picked it. Though their answer didn't have all the theological substance a mature believer would require, it gave me a peace in my child's heart until I got older in the Lord.

They simply told me that God didn't really care what flavor of ice cream I picked, and that He knew I would pick the Jamoca Almond Fudge because He's outside of time and had already seen my actions, much like watching a movie. I left church that night with a huge burden lifted from my shoulders.

A Closer Look at Sovereignty

Oddly, the term sovereign or sovereignty isn't even used in the King James Version of the Bible and is found only once in the New American Standard Version. Though the arguments concerning the sovereignty of God go way back, the term became popularized by the publication of the New International Version of the Bible (NIV) where it appears 303 times. I am not severely criticizing the NIV translation here, just stating the facts. In fact, I use the NIV as my personal study Bible and love how it reads.

It seems the NIV scholars took the phrase *the Lord God* and translated it into *the Sovereign Lord*. This rendition of the Hebrew is really quite acceptable since the meaning of the word that is translated sovereign is an emphatic form of a word meaning *to rule*. Sovereign Lord actually carries more meaning for us in the English speaking world since *Lord God* is almost the same as saying *Lord Lord* or *God God*, since they are interchangeable to us.[1]

All is well as long as the definition of the word *sovereign* is absolute rule, as that is what the main use of the word means. But somewhere along the line weeds were planted in sovereignty's garden. The term came to mean *to be in complete control*—not only *over all*, but also *causing all*. This line of thought is actually closer to Islamic reasoning, i.e. *"Allah has willed it,"* than the teachings found in the Bible. Just because the Scriptures tell us *"that all things work together for good to those who love God,"* it doesn't give us the right to say everything comes from God and that He has predetermined it all to happen (Romans 8:28 NKJV).

Rebalancing the Equation

Many of the weed-like thoughts about the sovereignty of God

have grown in our theological gardens because we have removed the enemy, the clash of the kingdoms, and fallen humanity from the equation. It is time to put them back! Scripture clearly reveals a very real enemy who is joined by an array of principalities, powers, and even people who assist him in his mission of stealing, killing, and destroying. When these are conveniently left out of the equation, who else do we have to blame for all the atrocities happening around us? The non-believer often accuses a mean God for allowing such things to happen. Many Christians attempt to make injustices more palatable by saying they are the result of the sovereignty of God.

> *Without putting the enemy back in the equation, we are hopelessly left in the hands of a schizophrenic God.*
> ~

This view of God's sovereignty, however, doesn't reflect the obvious clash of the kingdoms as revealed in the Scriptures. It also doesn't take into account the final revelation of God in Jesus *"who went about doing good"* and was *"the radiance of God's glory and the exact representation of his being"* (Hebrews 1:13). From the very first time that Jesus proclaimed the gospel of the kingdom, a declaration of war was heard in the spirit realm between the kingdom of darkness and His light. This war continues to this day until *"the kingdoms of this world are become the kingdoms of our Lord, and of His Christ"* (Revelation 11:15 KJV).

Without putting the enemy back in the equation, we are hopelessly left in the hands of a schizophrenic God, who brings death and disaster one minute and mercy and healing the next. This line of reasoning not only assaults the character of God, but it also results in giving a horrible witness to the unsaved who are looking for answers and hope. As Bill Johnson puts it, *"If any of us did to our children what many are attributing to God, we'd be arrested for child abuse."*

Left Prayerless and Powerless

This distorted view of the sovereignty of God also gives birth to a prayerless and powerless church that thinks her job is to sit and watch the all-powerful God perform His sovereign plan on the earth. After all, why pray if God is going to do what He has sovereignly planned to do? Why lift a finger to help Him with His sovereign plan?

This gets really absurd if we look at the subject of salvation. From Scripture we know that God isn't willing that anyone perish. He desires that everyone come to the knowledge of Jesus and be saved. So if God isn't willing that anyone perish, are any going to perish? Of course the obvious answer from Scripture is yes. But how could this happen if it's not the Lord's sovereign will for it to happen? Did God change His mind, or is there a tad more to it than that?

By putting the clash of the kingdoms back into the equation, we are able to see the role the enemy plays as he wages war on mankind. Paul reminds us in his second letter to the Corinthians:

> *The god of this age has blinded the minds of unbelievers, so that they cannot see the light of the gospel of the glory of Christ, who is the image of God* (2 Corinthians 4:4 NIV).

And what about man exercising the free will that God gave him to stay fallen? Choice was given to us in the Garden and it was never taken away, and we all have the freedom of choice to enter the kingdom or remain in our fallen condition. We may not like it, but the fallen can stay fallen if they want to. As C. S. Lewis aptly put it, *"A man can't be **taken** to hell, or **sent** to hell; you can only get there on your own steam."*[2]

The Lord's plan to redeem humanity has never changed. The Church is to take the baton that Jesus passed on to us and continue functioning as His Body in the earth proclaiming the *message of the kingdom*, praying the *prayers of the*

> The Lord's plan to redeem humanity has never changed.
> ∼

kingdom, and moving in the *power of the kingdom*. In fact, all biblical and historical revival accounts of heavenly invasions breaking into the earthly realms have come about by man co-laboring with a sovereign God, and it continues the same for us today.

The Old Testament gives us a beautiful picture of what it means for us to co-labor with a sovereign God.

> *See, I have given you this land. Go in and take possession of the land that the Lord swore he would give to your fathers—Abraham, Isaac and Jacob—and to their descendants after them...See, the Lord your God has given you the land. Go up and take possession of it as the Lord, the God of your fathers, told you. Do not be afraid; do not be discouraged* (Deuteronomy 1:8, 21 NIV).

Here we see the Lord's simple instruction given to the children of Israel for coming into the Promised Land, *"I have given you the land...now go in and take the land."* Note the theological tension that we are presented with here. We might want to reason that since He has given us the land, we don't have to do anything for it. This brings us back to our role in the cosmic war, the clash of the kingdoms, and co-laboring with a sovereign God to bring His rule and reign into the earth. *"I've given you the victory,"* says the Lord, *"but you have to draw the sword and bend the bow to take what I've given you."* [3]

Our Failures Don't Determine God's Will

One of the final weeds to deal with in this garden has to do with drawing conclusions about the will of God based on our failures instead of the life of Jesus and the Word of God. An example of this is found in Matthew 17.

> *When they came to the crowd, a man approached Jesus and knelt before him. "Lord, have mercy on my son," he said. "He has seizures and is suffering greatly. He often falls into the fire or into the water. I brought him to your disciples, but they could not heal him." "O unbelieving and perverse generation," Jesus replied, "how long shall I stay with you? How long shall I put up with you? Bring the boy here to me." Jesus rebuked the demon, and it came out of the boy, and he was healed from that moment* (Matthew 17:14-18 NIV).

Though there is much to be gleaned from this miracle, I mainly want to focus on the question concerning the sovereign will of God and the boy's healing. Jesus had already given the disciples the power and authority to heal the sick and cast out demons, yet when the man brought his son to them, they were unable to heal him. Though the text is silent here, I am wondering how the disciples handled this failure in front of the crowd that day.

It wouldn't surprise me if they responded to their situation a lot like we do today in the face of our failures. In order to save face or their own sanity, they probably drew faulty conclusions from their failure and reasoned that it probably wasn't God's will to heal the boy at this present time. Or perhaps they responded by explaining the complexity of the situation and that the Lord was probably trying to teach the boy or his father something through this illness.

Of course this line of reasoning ended abruptly as Jesus came on the scene and healed the boy. So we come back to the question of the sovereign will of God and the boy's healing. I believe when the disciples started to pray for the boy, they believed it was the will of God to set the young man free. As they failed to bring healing to the child, however, they began to reason within themselves instead of from what Jesus had taught and modeled before them. Of course the only conclusion that can be drawn after Jesus shows up and heals the child is that it was the will of God.

Let me end by offering two more brief thoughts concerning the disciples that day. The first is that they were disciples or students. When they were alone with Jesus that day, they asked Him why they were unable to heal the child. Jesus answered them by talking about prayer and fasting. This is the attitude I believe we should all have. We shouldn't lower our theology to the level of our experience. Instead, we should ask the Master to teach us.

Secondly, in the midst of their own personal failure to deliver and heal the boy, they frowned on those who were successful. The following is found in Luke's gospel shortly after the disciples failed to cast the demon out of the boy:

"Master," said John, "we saw a man driving out demons in your name and we tried to stop him, because he is not one of us." "Do not stop him," Jesus said, "for whoever is not against you is for you" (Luke 9:49-50 NIV).

This common practice in the face of personal failure needs to carefully be guarded against. Our failures should cause us to cry out to the Lord for more wisdom, understanding, and anointing, so we can also become successful and not tear down those who are accomplishing what we just failed to do.

In the next chapter, we will examine one of the greatest privileges the Lord has given to His children—co-laboring with Him through prayer.

Questions to Ponder

1. Can you relate to any of these weeds in your own theological garden?

2. How have you come to understand the clash of the kingdoms?

3. What do you understand about the sovereignty of God? Does He cause and control all things?

CHAPTER 14

CO-LABORING IN THE HEAVENS

In 1994 our parched and thirsty hearts were experiencing the wild and refreshing outpouring brought about by the Toronto Blessing. Though it was an incredible season of renewal and joy for many in our fellowship, it soon turned into the prelude for another paradigm shift the Lord was leading us into.

After about nine months of renewal meetings, the Lord spoke to my heart one night and told me to shut the meetings down. Greatly shocked by this word, I imagined what Philip must have felt when he was told to leave the revival in Samaria and to go into the desert with no further instructions. When I asked the Lord why, He told me that He had given us rain for nine months because our hearts were so hard. It was now time to break up the fallow ground so that we would be ready for the rain coming in the future.

What followed were two events that shifted us into the next season. The first occurred one day when I cried out to the Lord because I didn't know what to do. I told Him I had played my last card and had nothing else to play. After 18 years of pastoring, I had done all I could to grow the church and felt like I was at a complete stalemate.

Nothing could have prepared me for what the Lord showed me next. He told me that our fellowship wasn't His house because His house was to be a house of prayer. This hit me harder than anything He had told me up to this point in my ministry. My pastor's heart just broke, and I cried

> *We humbled ourselves before Jesus and asked Him to "teach us to pray."*
> ∼

out to the Lord for His direction. His reply was simple and direct: lead the church into a culture of corporate prayer and become His house.

On the following Sunday, I repented to the fellowship for not leading them into prayer and shared with them what the Lord had spoken to my heart. I personally didn't know anything about the kind of prayer He was calling us into. I told them that together we would begin the journey into uncharted territory and find out what it really meant to be His house of prayer. So with no books, manuals, or working models, we started at the same place that the early disciples did. We humbled ourselves before Jesus and asked Him to *"teach us to pray"* (Luke 11:1). I have always been amazed that the disciples never asked Jesus to teach them anything else such as healing or evangelism. Maybe learning how to pray Kingdom prayers is the doorway into everything else.

Though it would take another book to tell of our journey into corporate prayer, this supernatural prayer movement still continues to this day in our fellowship, and the fruit of it has surpassed my greatest desires for an on-fire church life. What follows in the rest of this chapter is what we learned about co-laboring with the Lord in the heavens through intercessory kingdom prayer. This type of prayer brought us into the realms of Heaven and established a house on the earth for Him to move through.

Moving Beyond Crisis Prayers

One of the most beautiful and disturbing quotes I have come across concerning prayer is accredited to Corrie ten Boom: *"Is prayer your steering wheel or your spare tire?"* It's not that our fellowship wasn't praying. It's just that for the most part our prayers were only spare tire or crisis prayers. They were simply a reaction to the schemes of the enemy and life not going our way. This type of prayer put our church in a defensive mode to the attacks of Satan and never moved us into the offensive role that Jesus and the New Testament church take.

As we began to embrace the paradigm shift of co-laboring with God in the clash of the kingdoms, our prayers slowly became our steering wheel and directed our fellowship into its destiny— to assist the kingdom of God in invading the earth.

The Playing Field of Prayer

Though intercession and prayer are far from being a game, let's consider for a moment that it is, and it's played on a field much like soccer or baseball. This field of prayer is a simple analogy that ignited and sustained prayer in our fellowship as we learned how to pray in alignment with the kingdom of God. We began to pray *kingdom prayers*.

1. Coming onto the Playing Field with Confidence and Boldness

> *In him and through faith in him we may approach God with freedom and confidence* (Ephesians 3:12 NIV).

> *The effective, fervent prayer of a righteous
> man avails much* (James 5:16 NKJV).

> *The wicked man flees though no one pursues,
> but the righteous are as bold as a lion*
> (Proverbs 28:1 NIV).

Because of what Jesus accomplished for us through the cross and His resurrection, we come onto the playing field of prayer with boldness and confidence as sons and daughters of God. Terror strikes the enemy as we step on the field clothed in the colors of our King and wearing the armor of God and His righteousness. We come to the field of prayer having a deep sense of honor and conviction that the One who calls us to pray, somehow, actually needs us to pray.

2. We Pray to the Father Who Is in the Highest Heaven

> *This, then, is how you should pray: "Our
> Father in heaven, hallowed be your name.
> Your kingdom come, your will be done on
> earth as it is in heaven"* (Matthew 6:9-10).

We come boldly before our Father to make our prayers and intercession heard. Here from the earth we call out to our Father in Heaven to bring forth an invasion of Heaven on the earth. As we will see in a moment, there must be an invitation from the earth to bring Heaven down. Prayer isn't calling upon a reluctant God to change His mind—it is inviting God into and through enemy territory so He can establish His rule and reign.

3. We Are in Enemy Territory

> *We know that we are children of God and that
> all the rest of the world around us is under*

Satan's power and control (1 John 3:19 TLB).

Again, the devil took him to a very high mountain and showed him all the kingdoms of the world and their splendor. "All this I will give you," he said, "If you will bow down and worship me" (Matthew 4:8-9).

Satan, who is the god of this evil world, has blinded the minds of those who don't believe, so they are unable to see the glorious light of the Good News (2 Corinthians 4:4 NLT).

When Adam and Eve fell in the garden, they handed over to Satan their delegated authority to rule the earth, and his dark kingdom began to rule in the affairs of men. The Scriptures and Jesus never dispute the fact that Satan, though stripped of authority through the cross, is still presently ruling illegally as the dark prince of this world. Though the church

> *We are in hostile territory...Satan is still presently ruling illegally as the dark prince of this world.*
> ~

and the earth belong to God (see Psalm 24:1), we are in hostile territory as we reclaim possession of what Satan has stolen from us and is rightfully ours. Through the privilege of prayer, we now reverse what Adam and Eve did in the Garden. Their freewill was exercised and it allowed Satan and his dark kingdom to come. Now we invite the rule and reign of King Jesus on the earth. (See also John 12:31; 14:30; 16:11, Acts 26:18, Colossians 1:13.)

4. Second Heaven

> *And you were dead in the trespasses and sins in which you once walked, following the course of this world, following the prince of the power of the air, the spirit that is now at work in the sons of disobedience* (Ephesians 2:1-2 ESV).

> *For our struggle is not against flesh and blood, but against the rulers, against the authorities, against the powers of this dark world and against spiritual forces of evil in the heavenly realms* (Ephesians 6:12 NIV).

This illustration offers a simple picture of the playing field of prayer. Here we see that the earth and humanity are in the clutches of Satan because he received them through deceiving Adam and Eve in the Garden. Scripture describes three different realms that some refer to as the first, second, and third Heaven. Directly above the earth is the first Heaven, the clouds and sky that are visible us.

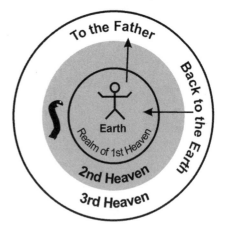

> **Look up at the heavens** *and see;* **gaze at the clouds** *so high above you* (Job 35:5).

> *When I consider* **your heavens,** *the work of your fingers, the* **moon and the stars...** (Psalm 8:3).

The earth shook, the **heavens poured down rain** (Psalm 68:8).

The Apostle Paul describes being caught up to the third Heaven:

> *I know a man in Christ who fourteen years ago was caught up to* **the third heaven**....*And I know that this man—whether in the body or apart from the body I do not know, but God knows—was* **caught up to paradise**...(2 Corinthians 12: 2-4).

From this verse, one can conclude that God does not live in the sky or clouds, but rather lives in the third Heaven. Father God and His heavenly host inhabit the highest Heaven.

> *The Lord is in his holy temple; the Lord is on his* **heavenly throne** (Psalm 11:4).

> *The Lord has* **established his throne in heaven**, *and his kingdom rules over all* (Psalm 103:19).

Now that we have established that there is a third and a first Heaven, it would seem logical to conclude that there is also a second Heaven. Although Scripture does not refer to a second Heaven by that name, it seems to describe a realm that is neither the natural, visible realm of sky above nor the dwelling place of God. Consider Paul's words in Ephesians:

> *As for you, you were dead in your transgressions and sins, in which you used to live when you followed the ways of this world and of* **the ruler of the kingdom of the air**,

the spirit who is now at work in those who are
disobedient (Ephesians 2:1-2).

I believe that the kingdom of the air is the second Heaven and the ruler is clearly Satan. The second heaven is the unseen spiritual realm where Satan and his spiritual minions, such as principalities and powers, have their habitation. When we talk about spiritual warfare, I believe that it occurs in this second Heaven realm, not in the third Heaven where God dwells and not in the sky or clouds above us.

Another excellent example of the playing field of prayer in the second Heaven is given to us in the Book of Daniel. Here we see what actually transpires in the heavenly realm as one of His servants prays on the earth.

> *Then he continued, "Do not be afraid, Daniel.*
> *Since the first day that you set your mind to*
> *gain understanding and to humble yourself*
> *before your God, your words were heard,*
> *and I have come in response to them. But the*
> *prince of the Persian kingdom resisted me*
> *twenty-one days. Then Michael, one of the*
> *chief princes, came to help me, because I was*
> *detained there with the king of Persia. Now I*
> *have come to explain to you what will happen*
> *to your people in the future, for the vision*
> *concerns a time yet to come"* (Daniel 10:12-14
> NIV).

On the earth side of the prayer, we see Daniel praying twenty-one days for wisdom and understanding concerning the word of the Lord given to the prophet Jeremiah. On the other side of this simple prayer we are granted a view into the heavenlies where we see a clash of the kingdoms. There we find the angel Gabriel being sent on the first day of Daniel's prayer from the third Heaven and meeting with resistance in the second Heaven realm as he encounters the prince of Persia. As Daniel perseveres in prayer on the earth, the battle in the second Heaven continues for twenty-one days until yet another angel, Michael, is sent forth to assist Gabriel and bring forth the answer to Daniel.

Though the Father's heart of love is for fallen humanity, He can't just *invade* the earth like some bully or vigilante and rescue us from Satan and his minions. He has to play by His own rules because He's also a God of justice and righteousness, and someone has to pay for the sins humanity committed. However, through the work that Jesus did on the cross, a foothold has been established in enemy territory from which God can be *invited* into the earth by the praying Church.

The same freedom of choice that allowed the takeover by Satan is now exercised once again to bring the kingdom of God to the earth. So as the Church prays to the Father, the Father hears and responds by releasing His angelic messengers to carry out his decrees. Though the angels may be met with opposition in the second Heaven by the powers of darkness and told they have no legal right or access to earth, their simple response is that *they have been invited*. This usually results in the clash of the kingdoms, but as persistent prayer and prophetic declarations are made, the kingdom of God soon prevails.

> *God can be invited into the earth by the praying Church.*
> ~

This is the honor and privilege that has been given to the Church—to actually co-labor with our Father in Heaven and invite His kingdom on the earth. John Wesley put it this way, *"God will do nothing on earth except in answer to believing prayer."* In the light of the playing field of prayer, let's read again these two familiar passages spoken by Jesus:

> But seek first his kingdom and his righteousness, and all these things will be given to you as well (Matthew 6:33 NIV).

> This, then, is how you should pray: "Our Father in heaven, hallowed be your name, your kingdom come, your will be done on earth as it is in heaven" (Matthew 6:9-10 NIV).

These verses relate to the gospel of the Kingdom. Whereas the gospel of salvation is limited to souls being saved, the gospel of the kingdom is the rule and reign of King Jesus being brought into the earth and all its kingdoms. Notice when Jesus teaches on prayer He is assuming that we know the *will of God* **is** *the kingdom of God*, which is modeled for us in the life of Jesus. Kingdom prayers are actually a declaration of war that invites the kingdom of God to come on the earth to undo what the enemy has done through forgiveness, healing, deliverance, provision, and other means.

Another example of prayer is found in the New Testament as the church gathers to pray for Peter who has been imprisoned by King Herod in Acts 12.

> Peter was therefore kept in prison, but constant prayer was offered to God for him by the church (Acts 12:5 NKJV).

Notice that the church didn't just lift up a casual prayer hoping Peter would be released but rather a *constant and persevering prayer*. This kind of prayer isn't trying to wear out a reluctant

God so He will change His mind concerning an issue. This kind of prayer comes by knowing His will, co-laboring with Him, and inviting His rule and reign into the earth. At its core, kingdom prayer is both intimate and militant. The result of the constant prayer offered on Peter's behalf is very similar to what Daniel experienced. An angel was released, prevailed over the enemy, and the mission was accomplished.

In the Western world, persistent prayer is usually hard for us to understand and embrace. One of the major reasons is that we have a distorted view of the sovereignty of God. Many of us believe that God is doing whatever He wants to do and nothing can stop Him. We are not convinced that our prayers accomplish much, and we completely forget the fact was God who taught us to pray for Heaven to be released into the earth.

Another reason why we fail to engage in persistent prayer is because we fail to see prayer as warfare, and we have taken the enemy out of the equation. We pray once for something, and if nothing happens, we determine it must not be God's will to answer our prayer. But those praying kingdom prayers already know God's will—on earth as it is in Heaven as modeled by Jesus. If we know it is God's will and we don't receive instant results, we simply take another shot at it. As seen in the last chapter, God has given us the land and we need to go in and take what He has given us. It is our privilege to exercise our inheritance and co-labor with God in the heavenlies through prayer. Jesus tells us to pray, pray, pray.

> *It is our privilege to exercise our inheritance and co-labor with God in the heavenlies through prayer.*
> ~

Then Jesus told his disciples a parable to

show them that they should always pray and not give up (Luke 18:1 NIV).

So I say to you, Ask and keep on asking and it shall be given you; seek and keep on seeking and you shall find; knock and keep on knocking and the door shall be opened to you. For everyone who asks and keeps on asking receives; and he who seeks and keeps on seeking finds; and to him who knocks and keeps on knocking, the door shall be opened (Luke 11:9-10 AMP).

God still holds to His original proposition:

Man is in charge on earth. If hell is allowed to take over, or if the flesh fumbles the ball, it's man's duty to call upon me for the remedy. If he doesn't call, if prayer isn't uttered, I have bound myself not to be involved. If prayer is extended, I have bound myself to conquer everything that would destroy or diminish my beloved creature, mankind.

There it is. Prayer can change anything. The impossible doesn't exist. His is the power. Ours is the prayer. Without Him, we cannot. Without us, He will not. —Jack Hayford[1]

In the next chapter, we will look at how we co-labor with God on the earth, which allows God to put us on like a coat and move through us.

Questions to Ponder

1. How have you come to experience the militancy and intimacy of prayer?

2. What has changed your prayer life from being a spare tire to a steering wheel?

3. How have you been able to employ the "playing field of prayer" in your life?

Chapter 15

Co-Laboring on the Earth

Five of us were gathered around a middle-aged lady who had crippling arthritis in her hands. Other than our desire to be authentic disciples of Jesus *there was nothing special about us.* We were simply the five that happened to be around her after John Wimber began the hands-on lab following his teaching session on healing. Her fingers were twisted and the look in her eyes confirmed what her husband had told us; she had been in constant pain for over fifteen years. Her actual age was only 54, but her condition left her looking like someone much older.

Though the five of us felt like "the ready, willing, and unable," the task before us was clear. We were to bring healing to this lady and undo what the enemy had done. So there we were, ready to take a risk, willing to fail, and knowing full well we couldn't do this unless Jesus showed up.

We had been in training all day with John Wimber at a Signs and Wonders conference. As John put it, it was our turn *"to do the stuff"*—to speak the words and do the works of Jesus. Though all that John had shared with us was straight out of the Bible, it still felt strange and awkward to put it into practice.

Somewhere along the line, we had ceased being little children—those true disciples who are eager to learn something new and are not afraid of failing. Though I am not sure how it happened, we became content with processing Bible information without putting it into practice. We had fallen into that pitiful state that James describes as *deceiving ourselves* (see James 1:22) and there was only one thing left to do. Now it was our turn "*to do the stuff.*" Knowing we were in a safe place—miles away from our homes and in an atmosphere charged with faith—we took the plunge to be students in this area of healing the sick.

We were used to praying to the Lord and asking Him to come and heal people, but now we were being presented with a completely different model. Here we were being told to move in the power and the authority that Christ had already given us. Jesus told us in His Word to heal the

> *Jesus told demons to go, eyes to see, and dead men to come forth.*
> ∼

sick, cast out demons, cleanse the lepers, and raise the dead. How were we going to accomplish what we weren't convinced we could do?

John told us to say the prayers and commands of Jesus. Up until that time we had never really noticed how Jesus had been "doing the stuff," only that He was doing it. But the Scriptures tell us He told demons to *go*, eyes to *see*, and dead men to *come forth*. Could we actually do the same? Apparently Jesus believed we could.

So the five of us began to do what we saw in the ministry of Jesus and we followed John Wimber's example. We spoke life over joints and ligaments so they would loosen, commanded the spirit of infirmity to go, walked this woman through unforgiveness and self-worth issues, and prayed that the Lord would fill her afresh with His love and His Spirit. We prayed for about twenty minutes or so and to our complete and total amazement she was completely healed of her arthritis.

We had actually co-labored with God to bring His rule and reign on the earth, and we would never be the same again. Though this was only a small beginning, it was all I needed to begin the journey of moving in the supernatural realm. To this day, I am co-laboring with God on a daily basis. God is a Spirit and is looking for people like you and I that He can move through to display His love and power.

Jesus Co-Labors With God

Once again, we see Jesus as the prototype for us in this area. Though we usually conclude that Jesus was healing the sick, casting out demons, and raising the dead because He is God, the truth is He did all these things as a man in right relationship with God and anointed with the Holy Spirit. But isn't that what all Christians are? As Bill Johnson put it so beautifully: *If Jesus did all the miracles as God, I'm impressed, but I'm not motivated to follow Him in healing the sick, because He's God and I'm not.* But Jesus didn't do any miracles as God. Instead, He models for us what it looks like for a man rightly related to God and anointed with the Spirit to co-labor with God on the earth.

Jesus gave them this answer:

> *I tell you the truth, the Son can do nothing by himself; he can do only what he sees his Father doing, because whatever the Father does the Son also does* (John 5:19 NIV).

Men of Israel, listen to this: Jesus of Nazareth was a man accredited by God to you by miracles, wonders and signs, which God did among you through him, as you yourselves know (Acts 2:22 NIV).

How God anointed Jesus of Nazareth with the Holy Spirit and power, and how he went around doing good and healing all who were under the power of the devil, because God was with him (Acts 10:38 NIV).

Here we find Jesus declaring that He couldn't do anything by himself. All that He did—the signs, wonders, and miracles—He did because God was with Him and working through Him. This is what He modeled to His disciples and expected them to imitate. This is God and man moving in tandem together. This is God with skin on, where He is the treasure and the power inside our human vessels.

But we have this treasure in jars of clay to show that this all-surpassing power is from God and not from us (2 Corinthians 4:7 NIV).

Now to him who is able to do immeasurably more than all we ask or imagine, according to his power that is at work within us, to him be glory in the church and in Christ Jesus throughout all generations, forever and ever! Amen (Ephesians 3:20-21 NIV).

The Disciples Co-Labor with God

The ability to co-labor with God to advance His kingdom on the earth brings us back full circle to restoring what Adam and

Eve lost for us in the Garden. This is the third and final step of the Green Ladder that enables us to act as His ambassadors on the earth to complete the task that Jesus started:

1. To speak the message of the kingdom

2. To pray the prayers of the kingdom

3. To move in the power of kingdom.

Let's look for a moment at some of the New Testament Scriptures that illustrate this concept of co-laboring with God in the earth. These are rarely preached, memorized, underlined, or included in Scripture promise boxes, but they speak volumes for what God has in mind for the Church. Most of these verses are found in the book of Acts which begins by stating: *"In my former book, Theophilus, I wrote about all that Jesus **began** to do and to teach"* (Acts 1:1 NIV). The rest of the Book of Acts is the record of what Jesus **continued** to do and teach through His Church, the body of Christ, as they co-labored with Him in the earth.

> *So Paul and Barnabas spent considerable time there, speaking boldly for the Lord, who confirmed the message of his grace by enabling them to do miraculous signs and wonders* (Acts 14:3 NIV).

> *On arriving there, they gathered the church together and reported all that God had done through them and how he had opened the door of faith to the Gentiles* (Acts 14:27 NIV).

> *When they came to Jerusalem, they were welcomed by the church and the apostles and elders, to whom they reported everything God*

had done through them (Acts 15:4 NIV).

The whole assembly became silent as they listened to Barnabas and Paul telling about the miraculous signs and wonders God had done among the Gentiles through them (Acts 15:12 NIV).

Paul greeted them and reported in detail what God had done among the Gentiles through his ministry (Acts 21:19 NIV).

This is to be the normal Christian life for every believer. It is why the Scriptures tell us that if the rulers of this age had understood what God had in store for His Church, they would have never crucified the Lord of Glory. Spirits, both good and evil, need bodies to display their characters and personalities through on the earth. That's exactly what God gets when anyone comes to Christ and is born again of the Spirit. Not only do we come to Christ, but He also comes to us, forgives us of all our sin, gives us His righteousness, and fills us with the Holy Spirit.

Now, as part of the body of Christ, we continue to speak His words and do His works in the earth. Through us:

- He shows His love through the fruit of the Spirit
- He demonstrates His power through the gifts of the Spirit
- He pleads for men to be reconciled to God
- He extends His forgiveness
- He prays and prophesies
- He wars in the heavens

- He heals the sick and casts out demons

- He feeds the poor and clothes the naked

Christ puts us on and wears us like a glove, and we put Him on also. We are clothed in His power. He is in us and we are in Him. This is the mystery that Paul proclaimed again and again in the New Testament and is the legacy of all the saints. Though often labeled as New Age thought, there is nothing new about it. This has been in the Father's heart since the creation of Adam. Though it was quickly lost in the fall, God's original plan stands firm and is finding fulfillment today in the Church as He continues to make man in His own image and likeness.

For those God foreknew he also predestined to be conformed to the likeness of his Son, that he might be the firstborn among many brothers (Romans 8:29 NIV).

We actually become the will of God looking for a place to happen.

Co-laboring with God in the heavens and the earth is the work of all the saints. From Genesis to Revelation, Heaven invades earth when man co-labors with our sovereign God, and it is the same for us today. He starts by moving us to seek His kingdom first in every area of our life and in every segment of society around us. He then puts us on to proclaim the good news of the kingdom and to pray that it comes to the earth. He empowers us with His Spirit to advance His kingdom by demonstrating His love and power. We actually become the will of God looking for a place to happen. And once our eyes are open to the kingdom of God, there are plenty of places on the earth longing and ready for Heaven to be established.

Today, I went to the store to run an errand. There was nothing big or spectacular about my errand or my day. It was just another day in the kingdom. While heading to the entrance of the store, I prayed that I would be filled with His presence so that I could *leak out* on people. I passed a lady in the parking lot smoking a cigarette and simply said hello. She responded by saying that she knew she shouldn't be smoking. What? Where did that come from? All I said was hello.

> *We seek it, proclaim it, pray it, and the Lord confirms His word with signs and wonders. This is Christianity...*
>
> ∼

I sensed that this was a good place for the kingdom to be advanced. After sharing a few kingdom stories to build her faith and expectation, I asked if she would like some prayer. She said, "Yes," and soon the power of God came on her. We were standing in the parking lot and she started trembling, telling me she had shivers all over her body. I told her that it was okay and that Jesus was setting her free by replacing the addiction to cigarettes with His calming and comforting presence. She then asked me where I go to church and the times of the services. I gave her the details and said goodbye. I continued on to complete my errand, thanking the Lord that He worked through me, and He thanked me for letting Him "put me on."

> *Then the disciples went out and preached everywhere, and the Lord worked with them and confirmed his word by the signs that accompanied it* (Mark 16:20 NIV).

Today, we are the disciples of the King and His kingdom. We seek it, proclaim it, pray it, and the Lord confirms His word with signs and wonders. This is Christianity—sons and daughters of God capturing His heart and love for the nations, co-laboring with Him in the heavens and on the earth, and advancing His kingdom on this dark planet.

I want to share two quotes from two of the generals in the body of Christ today. The first is by Pastor Paul Yonggi Cho of Korea, who pastors the largest church in the world. When asked how he accomplished such an incredible task, he simply answered, *"I pray; I obey."*

A similar thought comes from Pastor Jackson Senyonga who oversees an incredible work in Uganda and was featured on the incredible video *Transformations 2—The Glory Spreads* released by the Sentinel Group. When asked a question very similar to the one asked of Pastor Cho his simple reply was, *"Knees and feet, knees and feet."*

These two generals of the faith are examples for us today of what it means to co-labor with God in the heavens and on the earth. But it didn't start with these simple and brief quotes. It started when they embraced the gospel of the kingdom and their identity in Christ as seen in the first two steps of the Green Ladder. Even though much has been preached and written on these two subjects in the last twenty years, these foundations are not to become ends in themselves. These are the foundations that the Spirit is building upon in our day to empower the body of Christ to rise up and do what He's commissioned us to do— the very works of Jesus that advance the kingdom of God and transform nations.

In the next chapter we will review the three paradigm shifts. We will see how the steps on the Green Ladder build on each other so that the Church is ready to be used by the Lord to transform the earth.

Questions to Ponder

1. Share a time that you co-labored with God to advance His Kingdom. What was the result?

2. How has God confirmed His word through you with signs following?

3. Are you finding yourself beginning to look for opportunities to advance the kingdom of God in the earth?

CHAPTER 16

THE INCREASE
OF HIS GOVERNMENT

In the 1990s I was fascinated by the Magic Eye books that had astounded the world with what is known as "stereograms." These are 2D image pictures that have a 3D image hidden in them. The viewer has to focus their eyes just right to see the 3D image pop out. Stereograms are incredibly frustrating at first, but they turn into amazing entertainment when the 3D image is finally revealed. At first, you're staring at a picture with lots of splashes of color, boring to look at and depicting absolutely nothing. People are telling you there's a 3D picture of a lion though, and after looking at it for ten minutes or more, you think they are all crazy. They keep telling you to move closer to the picture until it's a blur, cross your eyes a little, and stare *through* the picture as you slowly move it away from you.

Just about the time you think they are all playing a cruel joke on you and you are feeling like an idiot for believing them, you suddenly see an incredible image of a beautiful 3D lion appear that is somehow standing off the page. What you have just experienced is a miniature paradigm shift—you just saw something that you couldn't see moments earlier. Amazed by this discovery, you turn to the next page and find yourself able to find the next hidden picture much faster, and the page after that is faster yet. Such is the nature of a paradigm shift. It gets easier and more real as you put it into practice.

The Restoration of the Green Ladder

When I first saw the Green Ladder in the dream, one of the questions I posed was why we didn't just build or buy a new one? But the dream wasn't about building a ladder. It was about restoring a ladder that already existed in the shed. It was there all the time; we just weren't using it. The three paradigm shifts covered in this book are the three steps of the ladder. None of them were new, nor had to be built. They just had to be *seen* or *realized*, much like the 3D lion in the story.

The ladder in the dream was put out of service and placed in the shed because religious reasoning had caked on and dried the mud of traditions and customs, control and fear, and greed and power. But this didn't happen overnight. It was a slow process. It was hundreds of years before the powerful church that turned the world upside down in the book of Acts fell into the dark ages where it was stripped of truth, became void of power, and was left with only a form of godliness.

But our God is a god of restoration and has been slowly rebuilding His glorious Church in the earth so that the gates of hell won't be able to prevail against it. From Martin Luther to the present, God has been in the process of restoring His Church by giving ordinary men fresh messages. These messages have given birth to extraordinary movements that have revived the Church and changed the course of history. What the Church needs to understand is that there's no Plan B. God is not waiting for the wisdom of man to come on the scene and *remodel* His Church. He's waiting for man to wait upon Him and capture His wisdom to *restore* the Church.

This wisdom of man is seen in the dream as I tried to use the sharp metal tool to remove the caked-on mud. As brilliant as the idea was, it had very little effect upon the ladder because it was only the fruit of my natural mind and reasoning powers. Even though some may have commended me for trying to remove the mud this way and may have even joined me in the cause, it was never God's plan. His plan is that we would work smarter and not just harder, using the tools of the Spirit and Word, and find the ancient paths that He has hidden for us in the Word.

> *His plan is that we would work smarter and not just harder, using the tools of the Spirit and Word.*

The religious mud in the dream was finally removed when the water of the Word and the Spirit came together and washed it away. These were the tools that Martin Luther and John Wesley used to restore justification by faith and sanctification to the Church. Later, William Seymour used them to restore the Baptism of the Holy Spirit to the church.

Others, too numerous to mention, used these same tools to restore worship and praise, the priesthood of believers, physical healing, the gifts of the Spirit, prayer and intercession, and other truths to the body. Even as these words are being written today, God is raising up other men and women to recover and restore long neglected and hidden truths to the body of Christ.

My prayer for this book, and indeed the driving force behind it, is that it will take you from mere information to restoration.

Hopefully, the many Scriptures, stories, and illustrations will begin to loosen and wash away some of the religious mud that has been slowly building up in the lives of many saints.

Some of you will experience immediate paradigm shifts as the words in this book will give language to something you have felt in your spirit for a long time but were unable to articulate. Others, feeling the tug of the Holy Spirit, will set aside their theological box for a season and search the Scriptures like the noble Bereans, staring and gazing into the Word until a shift happens—like seeing a 3D lion pop from the page.

Either way, eternal seeds have been planted in your hearts. When germinated, these seeds have the power to open the eyes of your heart and give you an understanding of the gospel of the kingdom, your identity as a child of God, and your destiny to co-labor with Him.

The Green Ladder Is Alive and Growing

Part of the mystery of the Green Ladder is that it's actually alive and growing. Though it appears at first to be a seemingly small stepladder, it has the unique ability to grow and increase as we begin to make use of it. Such is the nature of revelation that the Lord brings our way. As long as we continue to use it, it just keeps growing and expanding with apparently no end in sight.

It's like driving up an extremely tall mountain on a road that winds around the mountain like a corkscrew. Say an entire section of the mountain, from ground level to the top, represented the *love of God*. Each time you drove around the mountain you'd hit that *love of God* section again, but each time you would be a little higher up and experience a greater depth to it. That's exactly what the three paradigm shifts covered in the book are like. Suppose we split the mountain into three pie sections—one for each of the paradigm shifts. Every time we drove around the mountain we would have a greater understanding of the gospel of the kingdom, our identity in Christ, and our ability to co-labor with the sovereign God.

The individual steps of the Ladder not only grow in height and depth, but they also expand in width when they are put into relationship with each other. The concept of the kingdom actually expands when it's connected to identity and co-laboring. Identity expands when it's connected to co-laboring and the kingdom. Co-laboring expands when it's connected to the kingdom and identity. The three steps of the Ladder feed off of each other. As you step into the revelation of one, it releases more revelation to step into the other two.

For instance, my understanding of the gospel of the kingdom has dramatically changed and grown since I first heard it proclaimed by John Wimber back in 1982. Though the obvious reason for this growth is that it has been growing in my life for 26 years, it has also grown because my identity and destiny to co-labor with God have also been growing and are uniquely connected to the message of the kingdom of God. The bottom line is that God designed this Ladder to be used again and again. With each use, the revelation grows more and more and more.

The good news is that Jesus is the prototype for all of us, and He lived His life by using the revelations in the Green Ladder. The kingdom was His message and life. His identity was secure in His Father, and He moved in perfect tandem with God in bringing the kingdom to earth. He now calls us to arise and follow Him up and down the Ladder, until the kingdoms of this world become the kingdoms of our God, and we find ourselves changed from glory to glory, conformed into His image.

Arise, shine, for your light has come, and the glory of the LORD rises upon you. See, darkness covers the earth and thick darkness is over the peoples, but the LORD rises upon you and his glory appears over you. Nations will come to your light, and kings to the brightness of your dawn (Isaiah 60:1-3 NIV).

*For to us a child is born, to us a son is given, and the government will be on His shoulders. And He will be called Wonderful Counselor, Mighty God, Everlasting Father, Prince of Peace. **Of the increase of His government and peace there will be no end...** (Isaiah 9:6-7 NIV).*

I've saved the last chapter to highlight some of the fruit of the Green Ladder. After all, God isn't glorified in the seed or the tree, but in the fruit that the tree brings forth.

Questions to Ponder

1. After reading the Green Ladder, what specific shifts have transpired in your thinking and life?

2. Are you seeing the difference between God restoring His church and man remodeling it?

3. What is some of the caked on religious mud that the Word and the Spirit are currently removing from your life?

CHAPTER 17

THE FRUIT OF
THE GREEN LADDER

Though I have had the honor of pastoring the Vineyard Christian Fellowship in Grants Pass, Oregon since 1976, the first paradigm shift of the Green Ladder didn't come to us until 1982, when I first heard John Wimber teach the gospel of the kingdom. Since then we have also embraced the themes of our identity in Christ and co-laboring with the sovereign God. We have witnessed the Green Ladder alive and growing in our midst. The result has been absolutely incredible as I find myself pastoring a church I never dreamed possible. Though I would be the first to admit we are not perfect and there are certainly areas of lack in our fellowship, the fruit that I do see is good and has endured for many seasons and is increasing. Here is some of the fruit that is vibrantly growing in our midst as we've endeavored to put into practice what has been covered in this book.

His Presence

His Presence is everything! Without the King, there is no

gospel of the kingdom. Moses placed a demand upon the Lord when he said:

> *If your Presence does not go with us, do not send us up from here…What else will distinguish me and your people from all the other people on the face of the earth?* (Exodus 33:15-16).

The presence of the Lord was also the driving force behind David as he positioned himself to bring the Ark back to Israel. Even though the priestly duties were still taking place in the Tabernacle of Moses, the presence of the Lord was nowhere to be found. Such is the nature of all religion.

His presence was actually our first pursuit as a fellowship. It became our first reward and to this day it remains our highest value. Everything we need and desire flows from His presence.

> *As we go after His face, we also find His hands.*
> ∼

His promise to be a rewarder of those that diligently seek Him has been proven over and over again in our fellowship. As we go after His face we also find His hands. His presence isn't to be confused with claiming a verse in the Bible or believing He's here by faith. It's an actual and tangible presence that can be felt and experienced. His presence is its own reward. The fruit of His presence drops down into every area of our lives and the fellowship.

It's not uncommon to see people sit and weep during our worship times and tell us later that the love of God fell on them like a blanket. One of our leaders was a recipient of this blanket of love. He had been an associate minister for years in several fellowships and had faithfully served in many capacities, but he had grown disillusioned with the tediousness of church. After hearing several stories about our fellowship, he and his wife visited one day, and they both experienced a fresh encounter with the love of God. Healing tears flowed freely as he received a prophetic word from a child and healing in his hip. For weeks after, he continued to openly cry when he felt the refreshing presence of God.

His presence is the very atmosphere of Heaven that fills us with joy and hope, mercy and grace, acceptance and forgiveness, and tells us nothing is impossible as He proclaims freedom. These characteristics aren't just words; they are manifested every time we gather through tears, laughter, dancing, waving of banners, and in the way people extend grace that covers each other's faults and differences.

The Fruit of Love—A House of Honor

As we bathe in the presence of His love and receive all that we need from Him, we have plenty to extend to others in need. This incredible exchange of love He has given has created a house of honor for us. Our church is a house where religious control and manipulation have been replaced with love, honor, trust, loyalty, and respect. It's a place where we accept one another just as we are and where we are in our journey with God.

One of the most amazing characteristics of the house of honor is that we have come to believe that it is the Father's job to raise His children and not that of church leadership. We haven't done away with our

> *In a house of honor, we learn to nurture and guard the relationship with the Father more than the rules of the house.*
> ~

leaders or spiritual moms and dads, but we are putting the Father at the head of our family. We also trust that each person who is really His child and born again wants to know their Father and wants to pursue this relationship. In a house of honor, we learn to nurture and guard the relationship with the Father more than rules of the house.

We have built a prophetic community that further fuels our house of honor by speaking encouraging words that build up rather than tear down. Gone are the days of gossip, bickering, backbiting, complaining, and competition. We have learned to see each other through the Father's eyes and are catching glimpses of the gold He has hidden in each of His children—that unique deposit of Jesus that sets each one apart from everyone else.

In this house of honor, acts of love flow spontaneously out of hearts. People freely give away what they have received from the Father and are not driven by pulpit manipulation or programs. Our leadership team values having a safe place where people can grow up into Christ and that place is a house of honor. A prime example of the way that love and honor are demonstrated in our fellowship happened to one of our dear couples.

This couple has been instrumental in welcoming people into our church for over twenty years, and the wife has been battling cancer for several years. At one point, she needed to spend over a month in a Portland hospital for treatment. During this time, people in our fellowship rallied together to provide finances and labor to transform their home into a welcoming environment for her after her extended hospital stay. They cleaned and organized, painted, installed new carpet and laminate flooring, and gave the couple some new furniture to create a bright and cheerful home for them.

The Generations Are Connected

Over the years, one of the greatest byproducts of our house of honor is the connecting of the generations. As a pastor, this has to be one of the most fulfilling miracles that I have witnessed in our fellowship to this day. Honor releases life!

> *"Honor your father and mother." This is the first commandment with a promise: If you honor your father and mother, "things will go well for you, and you will have a long life on the earth"* (Ephesians 2:2-3 NLT).

I noticed a bridge forming between generations in our intercession meetings. The presence of God exhibited in these times of prayer was a leveler of our doctrines and social status, and it proved to be the same for age as well. During this season, our youth and children's pastors were bringing their young people into the presence of God and the supernatural realm of the Spirit. On the days we had children's church, the youth would join the children and serve as their teachers and mentors. The same thing happened at our youth meetings as many adults showed up to not only offer support but to join with the youth during their times of worship and ministry.

On one occasion, a lady in our church was experiencing excruciating pain from shingles and was in desperate need of prayer. The only meeting going on that night was the youth meeting, so she decided to go there and was instantly healed as the youth ministered to her. We began to see people in our congregation value what God was doing in each ministry and all of these events led us to corporately believe there is no junior Holy Spirit.

The connecting of the generations actually fuels itself—

continually releasing more and more life and love back into the body. It's not uncommon to see our children, teens, and adults connected together in worship, prayer, ministry time, service projects, outreach, and so on. It's not unusual to see our weekly intercession meeting sprinkled with many children and youth, and they are not just sitting there coloring or reading books. They are actually worshipping and touching the throne of God with the adults. Our healing, prophetic, and ministry teams that serve at the altar are also made up of a mixture of youth and adults. Little children often join in as they learn to minister powerfully among us. All in all, it has been an amazing journey to witness the Holy Spirit close the potentially destructive generation gap in our midst. We have become a house where a legacy is being lived, so that a legacy can be left to future generations.

Healings, Miracles, Signs and Wonders

In His presence is His power, and that is evident every week in our fellowship. Whether it's in a church service or the marketplace, stories are told each week of what our God is doing in and through His people. We see healings every week and many of them could be called miracles. Bones have instantly mended! Torn ligaments have joined back together! Pains that have hurt for more than twenty years have stopped! Ankles locked with metal plates and screws are now moving! Wrists with carpal tunnel are freed up!

Our youth and children have stepped out in boldness to exercise the gifts of the spirit and have seen many healings. Some healings occur when His presence comes in a strong way during worship. We call these "drive–by healings." One minute a person is sick and in pain, and the next minute he or she is healed without anyone praying for them. Many in our church are seeing angels, especially children, and incredible things happen when we act upon what these angels prompt us to do. Addictions have broken, depression has lifted, and hope has been restored. There have been visitations by warring angels, revelatory angels, and angels that deliver gifts and minister directly to people.

We have also had our share of signs that have certainly made us wonder. Some of these are seen in the Bible, some we have come to understand through prayer and meditation, and others have just left us wondering and pondering the mysteries of God.

Freedom to Become

The Scriptures tell us in Second Corinthians that there is freedom where the Spirit of the Lord is. Though this word has seen more than its share of abuse in the Church, we'll need to understand there is a vast difference between the freedom that originates from the flesh and the freedom that originates from

> *This freedom that flows from the Spirit has moved us from living in a culture of control to living in a culture of honor and grace.*

the Spirit. What we have come to experience in our fellowship for many years is the freedom to become who He's created each of us to be and to do what He has uniquely created each of us to do.

This freedom that flows from the Spirit has moved us from living in a culture of control to living in a culture of honor and grace. Gone are the days of creating cookie-cutter Christians where everyone thinks, looks, and acts like everyone else. Our small religious boxes have been broken, and we are dreaming again and finding our unique callings and destinies that will serve the body of Christ at large and bring about the advancement of His kingdom beyond the confines of our local fellowship.

This freedom in the Spirit has also caused a major shift in the role that leadership now takes in our fellowship. We used to spend our time thinking about church growth and planning what needed to be done and who we could get to bring that about, but now we operate as a living organism instead of an organization. Instead of calling people to be committed, we have given them something to be committed to—the King and His kingdom. We trust their relationship with the King to lead them on and discover their own God-given destinies. In fact, most of the new ministries, small groups, and services that arise in our fellowship come from individuals willing to take the risk to use the burdens, talents, and gifts the Lord has given them. The role that leadership takes in this process is to hear their heart, listen to their plans, and share good counsel. Simply put, we have learned to serve them to succeed and give them grace when they fail. As scary and risky as this may sound, we have seen individuals arise and birth some incredibly creative ministries that have served our local fellowship, the surrounding community, and the nations.

> *We have seen individuals arise and birth some incredibly creative ministries...*
> ~

Some of the small groups that have started from this process have focused on finances, our new identity in Christ, feeding the poor, serving meals at the rescue mission, learning to prophesy, and on new believers. One brother started a prayer chain via email where we have seen countless people healed and ministered to. One of our ladies stepped out in fear and trembling and started a supernatural children's ministry where kids learn to intercede, prophesy, heal the sick, receive words of knowledge, and hear from God.

Another of our ladies, actually my lovely wife, gave birth to a ministry in the Amazon Basin in Brazil. This focused mission has had a tremendous impact on previously unreached villages in Brazil and to our own fellowship as well. To date, she has taken fifteen teams up the Amazon River, touched countless villagers with the gospel, seen hundreds of people saved, healed, and delivered, and built nine churches.

These are just a few of the ministries that we have seen birthed in a house of honor, where freedom and grace have caused ordinary people to arise and do extraordinary things. These people have discovered why the Lord made them and are stepping into their destinies. There are young branches budding and growing in our midst. I'm sure we will discover more incredible kingdom fruit as time goes by and more people scale the steps of the Green Ladder to embrace the good news of the kingdom of God, discover their identity in Christ, and learn to co-labor with the sovereign God.

I want to end by leaving you with the lyrics from an amazing song by Brock Human found on his *Let Me In* CD entitled *Come Away*.

> Come away with me, come away
> It's never too late, it's never too late
> It's not too late for you
> I have a plan for you, I have a plan
> It's going to be wild, it's going to be great
> It's going to be full of Me.

Questions to Ponder

1. What gifts and talents has the Lord given you that you are ready to release into the body of Christ to expand the kingdom of God?

2. This chapter is called "The Fruit of the Green Ladder." What fruit have you seen beginning to come forth in your life because of the Green Ladder?

3. What have you had revealed to you in the Green Ladder that you're still longing to see brought forth into your life?

A Closing Word to Leaders

Though *The Green Ladder* will certainly help anyone who is hungry to move in the realm of the kingdom and the supernatural, I wrote much of it with pastors and leaders in mind. After all, you are the ones that God has called to not only tend the flocks, but to lead them into their destinies of advancing the kingdom of God on the earth.

We often hear unfortunate stories about hungry pastors changed by God at a *Signs and Wonders, Glory,* or some other supernatural conference and then going home and bringing upheaval to their churches. This doesn't have to be the case. Jesus himself told us not to put new wine into old wineskins for that very reason.

If you have gone to a conference where there was passionate praise and worship, an incredible presence of God, and a demonstration of the kingdom in healings and miracles, understand that what you just witnessed externally was built upon an invisible foundation. You tasted the fruit all right, but you didn't see the roots that produced it. No one ever looked at a building and said, *"What a great foundation!"*

And yet we all understand that without the proper foundation the building couldn't exist. The same is true of a spiritual building that houses the presence and power of the Lord. There are foundations that need to go down, before the building can go up. If they don't, the building will just fall over.

For example, let's look for a moment at the passionate praise and worship found at a conference. Often I see pastors conclude that they simply need newer songs and a worship band to obtain the results they experienced at the conference. But there is nothing magical about new songs and a worship band. Underneath the presence you would find passionate praise and worship. Underneath the praise and worship you would find a living faith expressing truths that were laid down on a firm foundation of the Word of God.

Hidden foundation stones had been set in place that could bear the weight of His glory and presence felt at the conference. One of the key stones laid down was probably the truth that all believers are priests and that the Lord will inhabit the sacrifices of praise that are offered to Him. There may have been other stones laid in the foundation that the worship team stood on, like the truth that God is looking for worshippers, that we can rebuild the Tabernacle of David, and that worship is a verb.

This is what the Green Ladder is all about. It is designed to change our foundation in three crucial areas that will enable us to move in the realm of the Spirit and the kingdom as modeled for us by Jesus and the early church—complete with signs, wonders, and miracles.

Though *The Green Ladder* is the first book I have written on what could be accomplished in and through a local fellowship, I have often joked through the years about writing a book on what not to do. For instance, in 1986 I had a great book written in my head entitled *Honey, I Shrunk the Church*, which came from a time when I took our church from 230 to 30 almost overnight. As painful as that season was, it had a great deal to do with the writing of *The Green Ladder* and why I believe the Lord is currently calling us to be a tugboat.

Sometimes our failures can teach us more than our successes, and learning what to do often comes from learning what not to do. Another thing the Lord made clear to me during that season in my life was that I didn't have to reinvent the wheel. Others had already walked through the minefield I was currently in and were more than willing to offer their wisdom and insights to me if I could humble myself and get out of my prideful know-it-all spirit. So I found the tugboats of my day and let them come along side me to bring me through the rough waters safely. Both their failures and victories have become my victories and I received a rich inheritance from each one.

So now it's our turn to be a tugboat to other pastors and leaders longing to get their ships out of the harbor and into the open seas of the Spirit and the kingdom. The obstacles are many. Sometimes they come from within your own life and fellowship, and sometimes they come from the treacherous seas without. Be assured there is a way through them so you can fulfill the destiny the Lord has for you and your fellowship.

One of my strongest values is recognizing that each fellowship is uniquely different. I also believe there are many things that my leaders and I can assist you on your journey. A few of these may include:

- Preparing for change, embracing those changes, and leading into change.

- Getting your vessel ready to leave the harbor. This

may include preparing a fellowship to embrace the incredible call that the Lord has for each of them and the paradigm shifts mentioned in *The Green Ladder*. It may also involve streamlining your current leadership and government into one of honor to empower people and enable you to move more freely on the open seas.

- Refusing to be a hireling pastor. Getting completely free from the fear of man (without making men afraid of you) so you can accomplish the task He has called you to.

- Learning to develop a simple leadership team based on honor that actually works and is fun. (I've had the same leadership team now for close to twenty years.)

- Establishing the worship of God and His presence as one of your highest priorities. Since He's looking for worshippers, let's do all we can to be found by Him.

- Creating a church for the Lord and His purposes instead of creating a church for the people. Move from being driven by needs and programs to being driven by His presence and vision.

- Coming to understand that there are biblical things we can do that actually God and establish His presence in our midst. We have a major part to play in this, and we ought to find out what we can do about it.

- Bringing a church into offensive kingdom prayers instead of prayers that are only defensive. (Prayer is the major element for sustaining a fresh move of

God in a fellowship. The prayers prayed today build the house of tomorrow.)

- Creating and nurturing a safe atmosphere of faith and risk taking.

- Equipping the church to move in the realm of the supernatural: enabling them to hear from God, prophesy, heal the sick, cast out demons, intercede, and so on.

- Creating a generational bridge instead of a generation gap.

- Promoting church services and meetings where God isn't only heard about but actually experienced.

- Learning to trust Jesus in His people and release them to fulfill their callings and destinies.

- Releasing children to move in the realm of the supernatural.

- Establishing a prophetic culture of honor where the Word and the Spirit come together to encourage, exhort, and comfort people so that they are valued for who they are and not just for what they have done.

- Developing a missions program that is relationally based. (This is awesome and has radically altered our church.)

- Establishing a financial culture based on kingdom stewardship and generosity.

- Honoring and serving the city-wide church and the body of Christ at large.

- Nurturing a safe place for people, and at the same time living in the tension of neither quenching nor grieving the Holy Spirit—even when weird things take place.

That just about covers it for now. I hope you have enjoyed *The Green Ladder* as much as I have learning and living it out in my own life and fellowship. To pastor a church I didn't even dream could exist has been one of the greatest joys the Lord has given me, and my sincere prayer is He will do the same for you. So go and enjoy the King and His kingdom. If you turn around and people are following you, that is great. If not, just continue to enjoy the King and His kingdom. You can't lose.

The best way to reach me is via email at: thegreenladderbook@gmail.com

Questions to Ponder

1. In what areas of your life and fellowship do you feel the Lord is bringing about a paradigm shift?

2. Are these shifts different ways of thinking or different ways of acting or both?

3. Since fruits come from roots, what part of your foundational structure do you feel needs to be changed?

Endnotes

Chapter 1

1. *Wikipedia*, "Tugboat," http://en.wikipedia.org/wiki/Tugboat (accessed December 7, 2010).

Chapter 3

1. See Isaiah 44:26; Jeremiah 16:15, 30:17-18, 33:11; Amos 9:11; Zechariah 9:12

Chapter 12

1. Brown, Driver, Briggs and Gesenius. "Hebrew Lexicon entry for David." "The KJV Old Testament Hebrew Lexicon."

2. Thayer and Smith. "Greek Lexicon entry for Iesous." "The KJV New Testament Greek Lexicon."

3. Thayer and Smith. "Greek Lexicon entry for Emmanouel." "The KJV New Testament Greek Lexicon."

4. Thayer and Smith. "Greek Lexicon entry for Ekklesia." "The KJV New Testament Greek Lexicon."

5.   See Colossians 2:17; Hebrews 8:5, 10:1

Chapter 13

1.   The Committee on Bible Translation, Life Application Study Bible: New International Version, "Preface." (Wheaton: Tyndale House Publishers, Inc.; Grand Rapids: Zondervan Publishing House; 1991), xi.

2.   C.S. Lewis, The Dark Tower and Other Stories: "The Dark Tower" (Orlando: C.S. Lewis PTE Ltd, 1977), 49.

3.   See Numbers 33:53; Deuteronomy 1:8, 1:21, 2:31-32, 3:3

Chapter 14

4.   Hayford, Jack W, Prayer is Invading the Impossible, 3d ed. (Gainesville: Bridge-Logos Publishers, 2002), 65.

Contact Information

For Speaking Requests

Or

Interaction With Steve Shaw

THEGREENLADDERBOOK@GMAIL.COM

To Order More Books

The Green Ladder
by Steve Shaw
Or
Love Revolution:
Rediscovering the Lost Command of Jesus
By Gaylord Enns

www.LoveRevolutionPress.com
info@LoveRevolutionPress.com
530-891-5599

Recommended Reading

Some readers of the Green Ladder may have noticed that, except for a small paragraph in the earlier chapters, it doesn't deal with the issue of love, which after all, is the greatest. My reasoning for not dealing with the topic of love follows these lines of thinking:

The first is more obvious to me than anyone else, and it's simply that the Lord didn't tell me to write on the topic of love, and so I tried to be obedient to write about the three paradigm shifts He told me address.

The second is that, in my thinking, the King is love and His kingdom is a kingdom of love. To talk about the rule and reign of the King in the earth is really the advancement of love itself.

Finally, I didn't write on love because it's already been superbly written about by Gaylord Enns in his book, *Love Revolution: Rediscovering the Lost Command of Jesus.* This is absolutely the first and greatest paradigm shift that needs to be made by the body of Christ in this hour. Though there are several books that I would personally recommend, this book goes beyond that. The Love Revolution is a must read. Get it, read it, put it into practice, and give the book away to someone else. Be the revolution.

JOIN THE LOVE REVOLUTION!

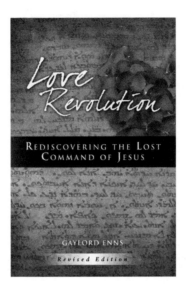

Get Ready! *Love Revolution* will rock your world. With its story-telling style, it gently pulls you in—but by the time you finish the last chapter, chances are you will be part of this revolution too.

It is one that will take you full circle back to Jesus, the author and finisher of the Christian faith. While Jesus taught us many things, He commanded us one thing. This book is about that one thing, its tragic loss and the imperative of its full recovery.

This is a message you can't afford to miss—one you'll want to share with your friends!

To order, please visit: **www.GaylordEnns.com**.